NINIA

AN ALIEN STORY

CARING FOR CANNIBALS

JOY DALE CRAWFORD

First Published in 2016

Copyright © Joy Dale Crawford 2016

This book is written in Australian English format.

All rights reserved. No part of this book may be used or reproduced by any means, graphic, electronic, or mechanical, including photocopying, recording, taping or by any information retrieval storage system without the written permission of the publisher except in the case of brief quotations embodied in critical articles and reviews.

For book orders and further enquiries contact:beracahbp@bigpond.com

Holy Bible Translations used: New International Version (English); *Allah Wene* (Yali)

'*The Swing*' poem by Robert Louis Stevenson © 1913 (public domain)

'*Four Things God Wants You to Know*' (ESV), © Good News Tracts. Used by permission. For more information, visit goodnewstracts.org.

www.merriam-webster.com/dictionary/alien

Stanley Dale and Patricia Dale's diaries and notes © 2016 Stan Dale family

All photos taken by members of the Dale family © 2016 Stan Dale family except baptism photo taken by P. Masters © 2016. Photo of Yemu playing jew's harp by A&C Clark © 2016. Photo taken after memorial service (unknown).

Graphics used with chapter titles: 1,4,5,7,8,9,10,11,12 and New Guinea maps: Shutterstock images © 2016

ISBN 978 0 9953760 0 7

National Library of Australia

Published by Beracah Book Publishing.

Cover design and typesetting by Lankshear Design.

Printed in Australia by The Word Print.

In Loving Memory
of
my parents

Stan and Pat Dale

who lived a life of exceptional
courage and commitment

alien

adjective | \ˈā-lē-ən, ˈāl-yən\

: not familiar or like other things you have known : different from what you are used to

: from another country

: too different from something to be acceptable or suitable

'Write what should not be forgotten'
Isabel Allende

Ninia

'I will remember the deeds of the LORD;
yes, I will remember your miracles of long ago.
I will meditate on all your works
and consider all your mighty deeds.
Your ways, O God, are holy.
what god is so great as our God?
You are the God who performs miracles;
you display your power among the peoples.'

Psalm 77:11-14

FOREWORD

Growing up, starting high school and dealing with changes in life can be a tough gig for any teenager. But it can be so much tougher when you are the offspring of missionary parents, and nearly all your childhood has been in the company of a stone-age people, where your schooling is done at home and your parents are the teachers, and where you have gone without all the mod cons of western society. Add to this the enormous grief of losing your father under the most bizarre circumstances that few would believe and then being suddenly thrust into a modern Australian society and school system and you have a deadly cocktail of issues involving culture shock, grief, self-esteem and acceptance.

As a youth worker and pastor for over 40 years, I have seen and journeyed with many young people desperately wanting to 'fit in', battling with the difficult landscape of bullying and rejection that is so prevalent in our society today. But the struggle for Joy and her siblings as they were catapulted into this new reality broke new ground beyond the bounds of normal teenage experience.

Here in this amazing story, Joy shares the simple delights of growing up in a native village high in the mountains of Irian Jaya and her confusion as her world crashed around her with the tragic death of her beloved missionary father and his friends. Her gentle writing style and fascinating story will warm and encourage you and give you hope in whatever struggles you are facing right now.

This is a book that is hard to put down once you start reading. The message in it is a timely reminder of the transforming message of Jesus, and the cost which has been borne by some dedicated souls in bringing it to others in even the most unreachable places on earth. Value the message contained in these pages and absorb it into your heart for the secret of happiness lies within.

IAN PURSE OAM
Pastor/ youth worker

CHAPTERS

1. Journey to a strange land — 13
2. Aliens do exist — 27
3. The Yali — 35
4. Stan — 41
5. Pat — 55
6. Everyday Life — 65
7. The Breakthrough — 81
8. Shoot to kill — 95
9. Good times — 109
10. Sad bad news — 121
11. Birthdays and deathdays — 141
12. The beginning — 151

PROLOGUE

The damp fog closed around me tightly, obscuring all but the fuzzy outline of the lonely grass hut or *yogwa*, as it was called. My mind flicked on a warning signal that somewhere nearby was a steep drop to the *Heluk* River, which flowed strongly at the base of the two thousand metre high plateau on which I was standing. I shivered as fear suddenly gripped me and I realised how alone I was. My daydream of claiming the abandoned hut and making it my own had given me a sense of independence, but now the idea left me feeling scared and wanting to retreat from adult thoughts.

From within the cold cloud came a comforting sound, a clicking noise followed by my name, 'Soy-e-e-e'. It was my 'big brother', Erariek, coming to save me. He cut through the white blanket of fog and stood before me in his stark nakedness, holding out his strong arms; a haven of love. '*Naut, nonggwelug yatma lahen?*' ('My younger sister, why did you go so far?') I felt nothing but safe as he gently took me by the hand and guided me back over the rough terrain to a more familiar dwelling.

Mother came to the door of our roughly built house with a look of relief on her face. The only thing she said was, 'Wash your hands, dear. We're about to eat.'

Later that night tucked up in my small camp bed, I heard my parents conversing, mostly grown up talk—the need to order more kerosene for the lamps and what information to give over the two-way radio the following morning. I glanced over to one side to see my younger sister, had already fallen asleep; her rosy cherub cheek resting on the lumpy pillow. My eyelids became heavy, my mind numbed, as I drifted in another type of fog.

Chapter 1

JOURNEY TO A STRANGE LAND

'Final Boarding Call!' boomed the loudspeaker, cutting short the quiet conversations being held in the cramped waiting area of the Wynyard terminal. A dark-haired man in his mid-forties shook hands with as many of the well-wishers as he could and then rounded up three small boys. A slender, attractive woman who was holding a warmly wrapped bundle of joy took her place beside them before the man ushered them all towards a door leading outside to the tarmac. The small group braced themselves for the cold wind and stepped outside. When they reached the boarding stairs of the Trans Australian Airline (TAA) Fokker Friendship, the family stopped briefly to turn and wave to the fifty or so people who had gathered to farewell them.

Dale family 1960

It was May 1960 and the Dales were about to embark on an adventure so different and strange that it could only be described as 'incredible'.

As the lush green island state of Tasmania disappeared from view, Stan gave his wife Pat, a reassuring smile and both turned their attention to the needs of their young children. For the two eldest, Wesley and Hilary, the first leg of the long and tiring journey, had a sense of familiarity. Both would be returning to the land of their birth. 'Well boys, we're leaving one island behind to go to another. New Guinea is much larger of course and divided into two. The eastern side of the island is a country named Papua New Guinea or PNG. That's where you were born. The western side of the island is called Dutch New Guinea or DNG and is ruled by the Dutch.

'Are we going to live in PNG, Dad?' Hilary asked.

'No, not this time, son, we're heading to the other side after we spend a couple of weeks in PNG.'

Stan and Pat were soon reacquainting themselves with old friends in PNG and took their young family to visit the mission station where, ten years earlier, they had pioneered the missionary work amongst the Wapi tribe in the Western Sepik district.

The day of departure arrived all too quickly and as the family waited at Wewak airfield for their short flight over the border to DNG, a casually dressed man together with a smiling lady walked over and introduced themselves. 'I'm Doug McCraw and this is my wife, Joyce. I'll be your pilot today. It's a fine day for flying so looks like we'll be in for a smooth flight. Your first time to Hollandia?'

After further small talk, the pilot got on with the task of weighing all the items that were to be taken on board the small Cessna airplane.

Pat stood nearby holding her baby and chatting to Joyce McCraw while at the same time watching the boys playing on the tarmac. Doug suddenly called out, 'Ah, bit of a problem here.'

His amiable wife wandered over and saw there was not enough room to put all the luggage in the cargo hold. 'I can sort this out!' she said with a laugh and proceeded to unwrap Pat's carefully packed items tucking them into every nook and cranny around and under the seats of the plane. There were things from Tang Mow's coastal shop scattered everywhere—bread, biscuits, oranges.

Less than two hours later one tropical country had been left behind, only to land at another further along the coastline. Despite all the mess on the plane's floor, nothing was broken and not one orange squashed; a testament to a skilled pilot and his efficient wife.

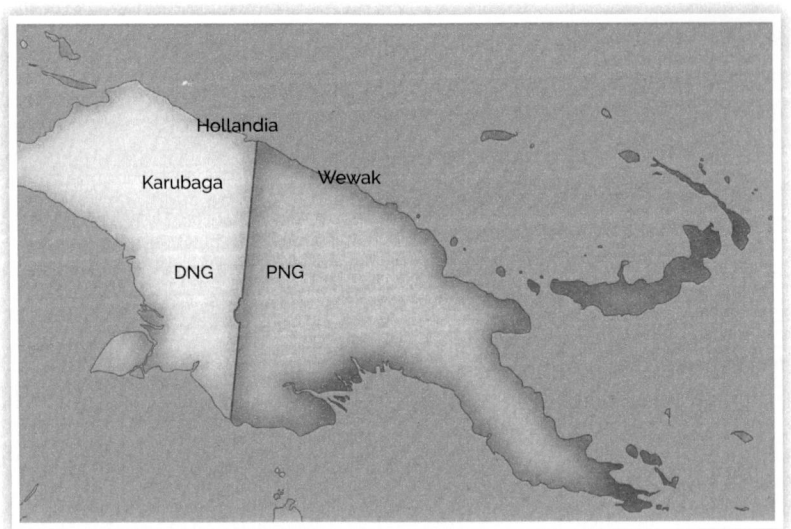

The airplane door swung open and the six newcomers were welcomed by a hot, steamy, tropical day, unlike the mild, temperate climate of Tasmania to which they had been accustomed.

After spending a few months of orientation with Regions Beyond Missionary Union (RBMU) near the capital city, Hollandia, the Dales were ready for their destination, into the heart of DNG.

Paul Pontier, a tall American man with an easy-going manner, sat in the pilot's seat of the Missionary Aviation Fellowship (MAF) plane with Stan beside him. The rest of the Dale family were strapped into the rear seats. Over the loud noise of the plane's engine, Stan attempted to be heard, 'It's good to finally be here. I've admired the work of MAF for years. You pilots are a brave lot. I hear that Betty Greene is flying in DNG these days.' 'Yup, sure is. She's MAF's first pilot. You'll meet her soon enough. She often flies the inland route.'

After soaring over a vast array of terrain—the swirling Idenburg River, the majestic mountain peaks, some of which rose three thousand metres up in the sky, and hundreds of square kilometres of untouched vegetation, pilot Paul brought his human cargo down to around fifteen hundred metres and soon had the compact flying machine bumping along the small hand-built airstrip.

Idenburg River

'Welcome to *Karubaga* and the *Dani* people, Stan!' Paul Pontier had by now, slowed the aircraft almost to a complete stop and with a sweeping motion of his hand, introduced the keen eyed Aussie to the unbelievable scene playing out just metres from the plane. Hundreds of dark-skinned, near-naked men, women and children, many smeared with pig's fat and soot lined the sides of the airstrip. As the Dales stepped slowly down from the aircraft the Dani people headed straight towards them like a swarm of bees. They pushed and elbowed their way closer, barely allowing the newcomers to move. Chattering in the strangest language, hands appeared from everywhere, trying to stroke or touch the white children's skin.

Two other missionary couples who were already settled in Karubaga waited for all the fuss to die down before introducing themselves. 'Welcome! Good to have you here.' Bill and Barbara Mallon and John and Helen Dekker had arrived in recent months from their homeland of North America. 'Let's show you where you'll be living.'

They led the new arrivals to a sizeable residence on stilts. The outside of the house was built from local split wood with opaque screens covering the small square-shaped windows. Inside the roomy building, walls were lined with a criss-cross pattern of bamboo. Roughly hewn boards made up the flooring. 'A plane usually comes in every Wednesday with supplies, so when you've settled in we'll show you how to order what you need,' explained one of the missionary colleagues.

Day after day the Dani people would come to the Dale's door speaking in their high pitched voices. Some of the bolder ones would take their curiosity a step further and open the door to stare at the newcomers. Stan secured a curtain over the doorway as an additional deterrent.

'They get down on their hands and knees to peer under the curtain,' Pat lamented. The lack of privacy was beginning to frustrate her. After one particularly trying day, a new idea came to her. 'I know what I'll do!' She went over to the doorway pulled back the curtain and popped out her upper dentures. The eyes of the Dani people widened with shock. 'Waaaaaahhhhhh!' they screamed and ran off. A few of the braver Dani returned for a second look at the white lady's magical teeth and one woman even brought five grubs as a gift. 'Maybe it's a 'thank you' for the unusual entertainment you've been providing,' laughed Stan.

'Stan, are you able to supervise the boy's school lessons and watch the baby for me today? I was hoping to give Barbara some help in the medical clinic.'

'That shouldn't be a problem, love. I'll be trekking the eight hours to *Mamit* tomorrow. The men over there have asked me to bring dynamite to blow up some of the large boulders which are hindering the work of the airstrip construction. I can finish my preparations as well as keep an eye on the children.'

Pat walked briskly along a stone pathway to where a small hut stood, looking like a lonely sentinel. Inside the dimly lit room were two wooden benches with several Dani people seated waiting for medical treatment from the missionaries. Barbara was already there attending a child who was listless with a high fever. The equipment in the tiny building was basic—on a table with unsteady legs was placed a set of scales for weighing babies, a stethoscope, some bandages, vials of antibiotics together with syringes; a thermometer, scissors, tweezers and cotton wool. Lastly, a large bottle of iodine complemented the supplies.

A sudden commotion outside caused the two ladies to go to the doorway. There in front of them stood a Dani man with an arrow protruding from his shoulder. Pat had tended to numerous wounds during her years as a nurse in Australia but never an arrow wound. Little did she realise this would be the first of many horrific injuries she would deal with in the years ahead.

About one year after their arrival in Karubaga, Stan and Pat were sitting together on the front porch of their home enjoying the calm balmy evening. The children were all in bed.

Stan was unusually quiet, then with sudden passion, voiced his thoughts. 'Since the arrival of more missionaries here in

Karubaga, I feel there are enough people in this place helping the Dani. We need to go and reach others who have never heard the message of Jesus. I know there must be time-forgotten people, walled in by mountain ranges, shut off from all knowledge of the outside world, passing swiftly to a Christless eternity, unknown, unsought, unloved.'

Pat nodded her head in agreement. 'As much as I enjoy the company of the other missionary women here and the comfortable home we have, I believe there is another place for us.'

Aerial surveys had been done on other valleys to the south-east of Karubaga and one in particular came to the attention of those who saw it from the airplane. Two rivers seemed to join at this particular location and the site was given the name 'Y' Valley by the missionaries. Surrounded by towering mountain ranges it would eventually be known by its real name, the *Heluk Valley*. Stan carefully examined the reports of the area and felt a deepening conviction that this was the place he was meant to be.

The 'Y' Valley

Stan's diaries:

> Some months later, I stood with a missionary companion and five Dani men who had consented to come with us, at the base of a vine suspension bridge that spanned the *Baliem River*. The vines and cane looked old and weather-beaten, the decking, made of split planks, tilted sideways and many of the planks had fallen out.

Bridge over Baliem

> Below it, the mighty river was constricted into a gorge about one hundred feet [roughly thirty metres] wide and the turbulent water surged down its steep descent, rolling restlessly over the huge rocks in the river's bed, filling the air with the thunder of its going. Across the river, a narrow track wound around the stony hillsides in the *Mugwi Valley*, up to the distant

ranges. The bridge looked a perilous pathway but it was the way we had to go, so we committed ourselves to it and got safely across.

Two days later we were camped in a village at the head of the Mugwi Valley. Far below us, the Mugwi River rushed violently down the Baliem and far above us, bare rocky ridges swept upward to the summit of the range and the clouds.

All that morning we climbed upward, breathing more heavily at the unaccustomed altitude, until we reached the top of the range. Suddenly, the clouds rolled in upon us and a driving icy rain forced us to shelter in some nearby caves.

After an hour or so, we persuaded our Dani carriers to continue and plodded on, over the boggy upland and through moss forest and heathland. Late that afternoon we pitched our tent in drizzling rain on the water-logged moorland and then looked around for our packs. They were not there and neither were most of our carriers who had, with their sure-footedness and speed, left us behind!

Without sleeping bags, dry clothes or food at an altitude of nearly eleven thousand feet [over 3,350 metres], we spent a miserable night. Finally, I went outside and sat down by the tiny reluctant fire and wearily waited for dawn. It came at last. Cold and foggy and with cramped fingers, we packed the tent and marched on.

About an hour and a half later we found our missing men sheltering in a cave and commenced clambering down the range to the far-off Heluk Valley. Then the fog turned to icy rain and chilled to the bone, we took shelter under a ledge of a rock, where we stayed for the rest of the day while the clouds rolled up ceaselessly from the south.

The next morning we continued down the mountain in the seemingly never-ending fog and mist, past peat-black bogs and through the dank dripping moss forest. The fog clung clammily about us and the line of carriers stole silently through the twisted, moss-draped trees, awed by the unnatural silence. At about midday the clouds lifted and we could see below us some cleared country. At 2:30 pm, we came out of the forest and climbed a rise to a village of several huts. We had come into the forgotten valley. Our journey had ended, our task had begun.

When we made known our intentions to stay in the area the carriers dropped their loads and commenced to sidle away, for a group of men had gathered on the other side of the river and they did not appear to be friendly. I advised my Dutch/Canadian missionary colleague, a single man by the name of Bruno de Leeuw, who had recently arrived in DNG, to wait with the carriers while I went on ahead. A narrow suspension bridge spanned the first stream and I got over this without mishap, then went on over a small ridge and commenced wading across the next rushing river towards a group of shouting men on the farther bank.

Yali men in the Heluk Valley

I could not understand what they were shouting about but their gestures were eloquent enough. 'Don't come here,' they were saying, 'Get out! Go back, go back.' It was too late to go back. I had not come all this way in time and distance to turn back at the word of men. It was not possible to watch the men and still keep my footing in the swift stream but I trusted the Lord to get me across. When I reached the bank most of the men had disappeared and those remaining had apparently decided to be friendly.

The next day men from the nearby villages crowded around our tent for a closer look at the abnormal intruders. [We later came to know them as the primitive, cannibalistic, *Yali* tribe] No white man had entered this particular valley before. The

Yali men stroked our skin, listened in wonder to our wrist watches and radio and curiously fingered the canvas of our tent. I made a quick trip further down the valley that day in order to locate the possible airstrip site we had seen from the air when we did the aerial survey some months previously. It was with some relief that I got back to the camp safely before sundown.

The following morning we prepared for a peace-making and friendship-making pig feast and an airdrop. About 9:00 am a little Cessna plane came over the range, circled to find our signal fires, then banked sharply around a ridge and swooped low over the tiny plateau where our tent was pitched, spilling out cargo as it went. Two runs were sufficient to complete the drop and the local men, who had watched in amazement, gathered around to see the strange things that had dropped out of the sky.

The third day after our entrance into the valley we packed our belongings and trekked further down the valley to the airstrip location. We arrived there in drizzling rain, wet, muddy and tired. I dropped my pack on the best camping place I could see, turned to my companion and said, 'Well, Bruno, this is it!' We were standing on a short ridge. At the lower end, there was a small hill which dropped at the bottom in a high bank, in the middle there was an extensive boggy area and there was another hill at the top. It seemed to be an impossibility to build an airstrip there with hand labour, but it was the only

> site in the steep valley that could even be attempted and families cannot be maintained in these isolated valleys without airstrips.

Sometime later the missionaries discovered that the local tribe had named this location *'Ninia'* meaning *'nini'* (ant) *'a'* (nest).

Chapter 2

ALIENS DO EXIST

Stan and Bruno asked one of their Dani helpers to try and convey to the Yali that the white men would like to buy some of the Yali land with salt and shells—the local currency. The Yali consented to this exchange but had no further desire to help the newcomers. They quickly retreated to vantage points on the mountain ridges surrounding Ninia, warily watching and waiting.

It soon became obvious to the small group that the Dani work ethic was not shared with this new tribe. Whereas the Dani had been willing helpers with the building of airstrips in their areas, the Yali saw no purpose in assisting these strange white beings and were pondering the meaning of why the men had entered their valley in the first place.

'Well, Bruno, it looks like we'll just have to do the best we can under the circumstances,' declared Stan as he picked up a shovel and with a look of determination on his face, began to dig.

Several weeks after the two men had left on their trek, Pat received a message from Bruno de Leeuw over the two-way radio, 'Pat, Stan is unwell with a high fever, nausea and severe abdominal pain. I've managed to contact Marj Bromley the medical doctor at *Hetigima* and she is fairly certain from the symptoms it's appendicitis. As you well know if left untreated, the appendix could rupture and Stan would become extremely ill and most probably die.'

More radio calls were made and within hours an MAF pilot named Bob Johanson was flying to the Heluk Valley. The stone-age Yali looked up in awe as the black and yellow Cessna plane swooped in low and another unusual looking man similar to the two who were now in their midst, threw out a package attached to a small parachute. The unfamiliar item landed safely nearby and Bruno retrieved it from the bushes then returned to Stan's side. The package contained the vital shots of penicillin which would be needed to fight any infection in Stan's body.

Some days later a doctor, who had set out on foot, arrived in the valley and continued to treat Stan for several more days. When he felt strong enough, Stan walked out of the valley and over the range at a much slower pace than when he had first walked in.

'I can see Tuan Dale coming!' shouted a Dani excitedly as he ran up the path leading to the Dale's home.

Pat hurried to the airstrip to see her husband walking slowly down a small hill heading into Karubaga. As he got closer she noticed him leaning heavily on a sturdy stick. 'You've lost so much weight, dear,' she commented after hugging him.

'Yes, I imagine so, especially as during those five days of merging in and out of consciousness, all I had was half a cup of water with a fly in it!'

MAF arrived and flew Stan out to the capital city Hollandia, in order to have the offending appendix removed at a better-equipped hospital. The operation, however, was delayed because of the state of Stan's weakened body. Four months later he considered himself recovered and felt strong enough to trek the now-familiar path all the way back to Ninia to resume working on the airstrip.

Stan's diaries:

> As I came down the range on the last day of my trek, the morning mist lifted and I could see the Heluk Valley spread out beneath me. A great longing came to me to hear songs of praise to God in that valley and to see groups of Christians in all its villages and I stood there for a moment and in faith, claimed the valley for Christ.

Heluk Valley

Building Ninia airstrip

Day after day, Bruno and I worked with some of the young local Yali men, who were now willing to help and together with the Dani men we continued digging away the hills and filling in the boggy area with many tonnes of rock. We had learnt again and again that the impossible can be attempted and achieved with the help of God, though we were not to know that it would take ten and a half months of back-breaking work before we shifted the two hills, filled in the peat bog, and got enough length for a light plane landing.

The completion of the airstrip meant the rest of his family could now join Stan in Ninia. Pat packed up their belongings, the children said goodbye to their Dani and Missionary Kid (MK) friends. The mild, warmer climate of Karubaga was left behind for a new adventure and life with the Yali tribe.

MAF checking the progress of Ninia airstrip

MK friends at Karubaga—Mallons, Masters and Dales

Crammed in tightly like sardines in a tin can, the passengers flew in the tiny plane to what would become a historic day—the first time a 'white' family would enter this part of the world. Navigating over high mountains and through narrow gorges, the MAF pilot skillfully landed the mechanical bird on one of the roughest, bumpiest, steepest airstrips on the planet!

Ninia airstrip and first plane

Looking around with a mixture of curiosity and unease, Pat's eyes came to rest on a gathering of men who appeared even stranger than the Dani she had left behind in Karubaga.

The men stood silently a short distance away, didn't smile and wore nothing except their *humi* (a penis sheath made from a dried hollowed gourd) and a necklace of shells. Their hair was worn in long greasy dreadlocks decorated with an assortment of feathers. Many of the men had pig tusks or bamboo sticks threaded through their noses. Most of the welcoming party were armed with bows and arrows. There were no women to be seen amongst them.

Yali men

The Yali had already had the experience of observing the two mysterious men, Stan and Bruno. Some of the younger Yali men had even been helping with the land clearing task, but this new and unexpected sight of seeing a white lady with four young albino-looking children clinging to her arms and legs, was indeed shocking to the locals.

Stan and the pilot unloaded the cargo from the plane. There were enough supplies to keep a family maintained until the plane returned in a couple of weeks.

The apprehensive newcomers walked slowly to the side of the

dirt strip and watched as the last link to the world they'd just come from, rev its engine, sway drunkenly from side to side, pick up speed, and become a tiny speck in the distant sky.

Stan gestured to some of the men to come and help carry the items from the plane down the hilly airstrip to where a humble abode was waiting.

He reached down to pick up his daughter as I reached up for the safety of his strong arms!

Chapter 3
THE YALI

On a steep hill overlooking the strip of cleared land, Yali women and children watched in amazement when the noisy *Suwe humon* (large bird) landed. Ever since the two pale beings had entered their valley things were different. 'Why do you think they've come here to us? Where have they come from? Our young men seem too interested in spending time with them and have already helped prepare the ground for the arrival of the Suwe humon.'

It was not the women's business however, to question their men over the bizarre changes. It was up to the men to sort out the meaning of life and deal with the odd-looking humans now in their midst. The women's curiosity was nevertheless aroused especially when the giant bird emptied out of its belly, not only the pale skinned man, but also an equally colourless woman and four children!

Yali women tending gardens

Homomak sighed. It had been a long day just as every day was long and tiring. She needed to stop digging and collect the *siburu* (sweet potatoes) she had already dug up and put in a pile. As she stood upright and stretched her aching limbs, she called to a small child who had been helping in the gardens. 'Hondoen, bring your *sum* (net bag) to carry the extra siburu and take my *kisim* (digging stick).'

The other Yali women in the surrounding gardens were also getting ready to leave after a productive day's work. This season's siburu crop had been a good one, unlike last year when the heavy rains came and landslides caused the gardens to disappear under a mountain of dirt and rocks. The hunger pangs had been difficult to bear and had it not been for the insects, birds and edible green leaves they occasionally found, many more of their family and friends would have died.

Yali woman with burden

On the return walk to their village, an important stop would need to be made in order to collect firewood from where their menfolk had earlier cleared land. Aside from the already heavy bag of siburu, Homomak carried another bulky bag which remained slung from her head at all times and was only set down once she returned to the safety of her *homia* (women's hut).

As the weighed-down women made their way to their homias, they passed by the *Ouswa Obam* (sacred hut) of knowledge. Homomak quickened her steps and kept her young daughter Hondoen, in sight. It would be tragic if the girl accidently went too close to the Ouswa Obam with the mysterious markings on its walls.

Ouswa Obam

Homomak remembered back to when her friend's daughter had been caught peering into one such hut. The punishment was swift and unstoppable. The poor girl had been dragged to a precipice overlooking the raging Heluk River and without hesitation, been picked up by one of the powerful village chieftains and thrown into the swirling rapids far below. The terrible memory still haunted Homomak as it did the other women but they dared not challenge the authority of the Yali men. 'We have not been given the revelation and meaning of the 'deep' things. Only the men have this important knowledge. We cannot stop what is meant to be,' they murmured.

The next day Homomak woke before the light broke through the sky. Yawning she raised herself to a seated position on the hard wooden planks in the upper section of the small round homia and looked over at her young daughter who was beginning to stir from her sleep. It would soon be time to leave again for their garden to begin the day's work but once more she would coax the dying embers of the fire in the centre of the homia. On one side of the small fire pit were a couple of cold, cooked siburu. Homomak would share one with her daughter and put the other in her *sum* so they would have something to eat later in the day.

A familiar whimpering sound grew into a steady cry and Homomak shifted her attention from the fire to a *sum* nearby. She made a gentle clicking noise to soothe the young baby lying inside the string bag on a flattened bed of leaves. 'Shhh, my little one,' she whispered, 'come'. Carefully she lifted her baby boy and held him close as he suckled from her.

Using her free hand she poked at the fire with a stick before looking up to see her daughter wrapping a small *kembalek* (a tiny skirt made from dried reeds) around her thin hips. 'Will I let the pigs out?' she asked her mother. '*Yu'o* (yes) and tell your father we are going to the gardens soon. If he is not in his *yogwa* (men's hut) he may be with his other wife. Look for him at her homia.'

Four small pigs began to squeal in their sectioned part of the homia as Hondoen removed the wood from the entrance of the hut and both girl and pigs stepped out of the smoky enclosure and into the fresh morning air. The piglets ran around, happy to be free of their confinement.

Hondoen looked up and saw her father, Dongla, coming down the dirt path and waited until he was near enough before repeating her mother's words. The man looked at his daughter briefly but didn't initiate a conversation instead he went to check on his important pigs, for without pigs, his family would have no social status and nothing to contribute to the important ceremonies in life.

Homomak with the sleeping baby slung in the *sum* on her back, walked out of their village with Hondoen beside her. They began the steep climb to the gardens but suddenly Homomak stopped and looked over at the cleared land to where the strangers had taken up residence in the unfamiliar dwelling. There she saw three young boys and one of them was chasing a small female child around in circles. The sound of children laughing was not unheard of in the Yali world but what caught her eye were the male and female adults. *They* were also laughing and even more strangely, had their arms around one another!

With a mixture of nervousness, bewilderment and curiosity, Homomak silently asked herself the question every female in Ninia had been thinking, '*It enahap kuron su sanim?*' ('Who are these white-skinned people?')

Chapter 4

STAN

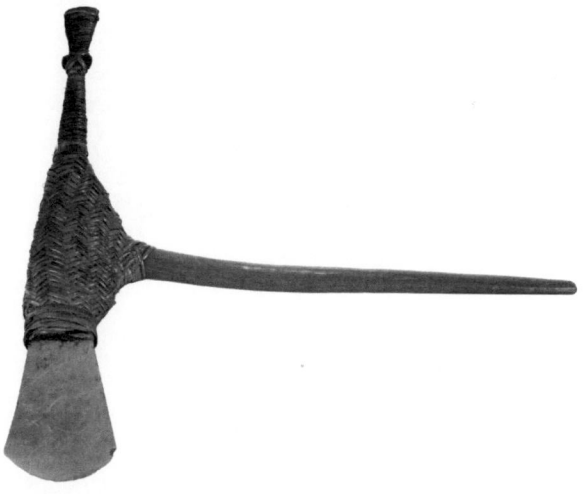

T he sight of our new home in Ninia did nothing to alleviate Mum's concern. She stared at it with shock. A grass hut barely big enough for two people, let alone a family of six, stood in front of her.

Pat and children outside their Ninia hut

Peering into the dim interior she noticed the dirt floor. 'Oh, Stan, I thought we'd at least have a home more substantial than this!'

'There is a second small hut over there dear, and we could use that as well.'

Mum looked around slowly before speaking again. 'Come on children, let's get unpacked.' Inside the gloomy hut it became obvious that there was no storage space so being the resourceful person she was, Mum found a clean rice bag for each of us for our belongings. Camp beds were soon set up and the rest of the day was spent organising our limited possessions.

The following morning light pierced its way through the cracks in our rough shack and one by one we woke.

'May we go outside and play for a while, Mum?' Rod was eager to see more of his new surroundings. Wes and Hil also wanted to explore the unusual landscape. 'Yes, I think that's a fine idea.' Dad looked up from checking the battery on the radio we would use to maintain contact with the outside world. 'We need to get a fire going and start breakfast before planning our day.' Mum nodded. She was keen to get the two eldest boys straight back into their school lessons but first there would be time to stretch our legs.

In single file we stepped out through the rickety door of our hut and stood silently surveying our new surroundings. A short distance away was the dirt airstrip with a lonely windsock hanging limp at the farthest end near the drop to the Heluk River. At the top section of the airstrip was a steep mountain where one side had obviously been cleared and cultivated and garden beds now sat waiting for their workers to arrive.

'Come on Joy, I'll chase you!' smiled Hil and started to run towards me. I laughed and ran as fast as I could away from him not realising that all I was really doing was running in circles. Mum stood together with Dad, his arm around her shoulders. Both were laughing.

Each day had its own challenges whether it was collecting water from the river at the base of the plateau our huts were perched on, or keeping a fire lit.

'Stan, we need more firewood.' Mum sounded frustrated as she viewed the meagre supply next to our grass hut.

'I know dear, but I'm finding it difficult to get any as every branch and tree seems to be owned by someone and they are reluctant to part with anything but a few green sticks. I have offered salt and shells but maybe I need to try and bulk-buy some wood in exchange for an axe.'

'It's worth a try. They seem to covet the steel axe we have.'

The following day my dad managed to convey the idea to Dongla, the village chief, that he could take the axe and keep it if a suitable amount of wood was left behind.

One of our most valued possessions was a forty-four gallon drum. Dad cut this drum in two and half was used to store our water and the other half was used for cooking purposes until a cast iron stove could be flown in from the coast.

The months passed quickly and life became a busy routine of Dad trying to learn the Yali language while at the same time attempting to build a more suitable house for his family. Mum too, had her hands full with domestic work and supervising Wesley, Hilary, and Rodney's school correspondence lessons.

A break in the routine would occur whenever MAF flew in to bring supplies or mail and packages from Australia.

More Yali men started to 'drop by' our home since learning of the Chief's axe payment. They sat on the ground near our hut and carefully watched the mysterious family who seemed to do the strangest things. 'Why do they cover their bodies with those coloured skins and did you see their feet? They put some kind of animal's feet on top of their own. It's all so unnatural!' The men seemed bemused at the lifeless baby I carried around all day.

Joy showing Yali man her doll

Dongla became a regular visitor to our home. One day he was accompanied by a small female child with a distended stomach and very thin arms and legs. 'Hondoen', he stated matter-of-factly, pointing to the girl as dad and I came closer. Dad didn't seem too interested in the child who was standing to one side with her head lowered but I stared at the dirt stained skinny girl with the big stomach. She glanced up shyly and soft brown eyes met bright green ones for the very first time.

'Why do they have big tummies, Mum?' Rod later asked.

'It's probably because they don't have the right type of food to make them healthy, dear. Their stomachs are not fat, it just looks that way.'

Some of the younger Yali men seemed more accepting of us and soon became enlisted to help around the home and with babysitting me. I would be hoisted onto strong shoulders and grab tight curly hair with my small hands while instinctively hanging on and going wherever my 'carrier' went!

After spending a year in Ninia my two older brothers, Wes and Hil, would soon be coming to the end of their primary schooling and would need more focused teaching. It was a difficult time for everyone as dad and mum made the heart-breaking decision to send their two sons back to Australia for further education. Dad broke the news to Rod and me one night as we finished our meal. 'Wesley and Hilary are returning to Tasmania so they can go to school there. They will be living with grandma and grandpa in Nabageena.' [a farming community in north-west Tasmania]

Not long after we were told this sad news, my two eldest brothers flew from Sentani to Wewak, then to Madang, Lae and Port Moresby, all towns in PNG, before continuing the long journey to Brisbane, Sydney, Melbourne and finally Wynyard, in Tasmania. They travelled the distance on their own. Wes was eleven years old and Hil nine years. Two weeks before they left DNG, Indonesia took over the western side of the island of New Guinea and named it Irian Barat, or West Irian for English speakers.

Dad, Mum, Rod and I continued our lives at Ninia but our family was separated and things would never be quite the same again for any of us.

'Joy, did you make this mess in here?' my dad called out gruffly.

I struggled to open my eyes after drifting off to sleep for the second time that night and then pretended I hadn't heard his voice, but within seconds my conscience got the better of me and it also occurred to me that there would be no point in lying as dad, being the smart man he was, would soon have the answer figured out anyway.

A bad case of the runs isn't pleasant at any time, but I knew I'd have to trudge to the outdoor pit toilet in the dark, so I used a container which I found near the kitchen. Unfortunately for me, it was not large enough for the job!

'Yes, Dad. It was me. Sorry I couldn't make it to the pit in time.' I was also thinking, *no way would I have gone to the small outhouse, barely big enough to hold even me, in the middle of the night*. I was afraid of the tall Pandanus trees which lined the route to the pit toilet. Their swaying fronds looked like giant arms reaching out to grab me as I passed by.

The worst thing about the 'pit' however was that it had already claimed the life of my favourite teddy bear when I accidently dropped it into the smelly abyss one day.

By the following morning the gloomy damp clouds had dispersed and the sun shone with unfamiliar warmth. My tummy had settled enough to have a rushed breakfast of homemade bread and a cup of 'Sunshine full cream' powdered milk. With Mum's 'don't be long, you're going to start your school lessons soon,' I ran off bare-footed to find Dad.

I looked up in the direction of the loud, sharp sounds and saw him chiselling away on a roughly cut log as he continued to work on our new house. Feeling a little disappointed that it wouldn't be a suitable time to interrupt him, I walked slowly back inside to begin the boring task of writing on paper with a pencil.

Stan building house

Ships are required to fly their flags when entering or leaving a harbour … 'Why do I need to write about imaginary ships when there are so many fun things to do right on my doorstep?'

Wash day

'L*ohon nanggno hakin!*' ('wait!') Mum called, as she looked outside and saw one of the Yali boys who worked as our house help, 'Don't boil up my shoes! Rodney and Joy, take a short break.'

She hurried outside to save the shoes from being put into a large copper pot.

The sound of giggles and staccato-like chatter caused me to drop my pencil and run to the open door. I noticed Mum was now giving instructions to the two helpers on how to stir the clothes in another big pot. *She'll probably be a long time yet*, I thought.

With only a slight feeling of guilt, I hopped down the back steps and into the dirt where my best friend, Hondoen, her little brother, Otto, and a couple of other children were waiting patiently for the strange, pale-skinned *omalik* (child) who seemed to be held captive more often than not. We grinned at each other and ran off.

Once at the village on the other side of the airstrip, Hondoen took charge of our expedition. 'Come on, I know where we can find some juicy *Igusu!*' (grubs)

'Soy-e-e-e...' (the Yali had a way of extending the end of my name and using an 'S' sound for a 'J')

'Here is a stick for you,' Hondoen said, handing me one.

I took the digging stick made of strong bamboo and followed the others past the cluster of huts to a levelled section of ground. Hondoen gave us all a wide smile, her white teeth contrasting against the dark colour of her face. 'This is a good place to find Igusu.'

We plonked ourselves down on the ground and began our mission. Scratching in the dirt like a flock of chickens and with a look of deep concentration, Otto's sudden squeal caught our attention, 'I've found one!'

We all nodded approvingly and went back to make our own discoveries. *Squish...* I'd made contact with something soft and quickly dropped the stick and used my fingers to part the dirt more carefully. 'Hooray, I got one too!'

'Put it in your mouth, Soyee.'

I looked at the plump little white grub as it tried to curl itself into a ball and wriggle its way back to its dark underground life. 'It's wriggling too much.'

Hondoen made a motion of hand to mouth and giggled.

'Okay, here I go!' My teeth clamped down on the innocent life and there was a quick burst of slime as I began to chew. The others watched me closely. Not wanting to seem different from my friends I nodded my approval and said, 'Yu'o, good!' It wasn't long before the others too had been successful in finding a snack.

Somewhere in the back of my mind the thought came to me that I could possibly be in trouble and realised that I needed to get back to my lessons.

With my stick still in hand I tried to sneak back inside to the claustrophobic classroom only to see that it was Dad and not Mum who was now supervising the lessons. Rod had his head down busy writing.

I sat down quickly, exchanging one piece of wood for another.

He raised a questioning eyebrow at me.

'I was eating grubs with my friends, Dad.'

'Well, at least you've had some protein then. Righto, now that Joy's decided to come back we'll do something else. Close your book Rod. I'm going to tell you both a real life story.'

Dad crossed his arms, shifted his wiry frame and frowned thoughtfully as he leant back on the folding chair and began to speak,

'The three men moved cautiously along the jungle track, their eyes probing the undergrowth, fingers on the triggers of their weapons, ready for instant action. They were part of an Australian commando unit of three hundred men, specially trained in raiding and jungle warfare, who early in 1943, patrolled the Lower Markham Valley in Papua New Guinea. Opposed to them were thirty thousand Japanese soldiers based in the town of Lae.

'For hour after hour the tiny patrol climbed upward along a razorback ridge until they came to a break in the rainforest and they could look across the Markham River and the distant town of Lae. To one of the party, though, the thing of greatest interest was not the sight of the barges chugging slowly up the river to supply the Japanese outposts. From the lookout post at a height of three thousand feet, [over nine hundred metres] he could see a wide sweep of grassland shining in the sunlight, and beyond it, ridges and ranges that rose, tier after tier, cloud-wreathed or misty blue, into the interior of the great island of New Guinea.

'What lay behind those mountains? What people lived there? Had they ever heard that God had a son who loved them and came to earth to die for their sins? If they had not heard, how would they ever hear unless someone went to tell them of a Saviour's love? These were the questions that began to form in the mind of the young commando and slowly the resolve was formed that, someday, somehow he would go behind those ranges and bring to the people who lived in the unknown valleys beyond them the life-giving word of God.

'I was that young commando.'

Dad abruptly stopped and looked down at our desks. 'Now, where were you up to in your books?'

It took a moment for my mind to register that he was redirecting our attention back to school work. But neither Rod nor I had any interest in going back to writing down nouns, verbs and adjectives. I wanted to hear them all dressed up in exciting sentences. 'Aw, please Dad, can you tell us more about your life?'

He gave a lopsided smile and raised one of his craggy eyebrows with a look that suggested he knew when someone was hooked by his masterful storytelling. 'All right, I'll tell you a little more but then the two of you must get back to your school books.'

'I was born in a small country town—Kyogle—in northern New South Wales in 1916 and spent the early years of my childhood on a farm there. My dad, your grandpa, was a harsh man and an alcoholic. That means he couldn't stop drinking liquor, which is a fermented drink. Some people, like my father, can turn unpleasant when they drink too much alcohol.'

'Did you like school?' I asked.

He looked thoughtful. 'Yes and no. I enjoyed learning about lots of things and read as many books as I could get my hands on, mostly at the local library, but there were times I, well … sometimes when you are with other children you will find that some of them have a nasty streak. They're called bullies. I met a few in my time, but the important thing to remember is that you decide how you will respond to them.

'Sometimes bullies are the way they are because they themselves were bullied but you don't let them get the upper hand. Some children become so fearful of these mean-spirited people that they are targeted even more. I decided that the best way to deal with these type of kids was to challenge them at their own game; show them up for how weak they were and make them realise they couldn't control my life.'

'How did you do that?' Rod asked.

'I left them in my dust.'

'What do you mean?'

'I mean I concentrated on improving myself. I learned to outrun them. They could never catch me because I was too fast.

'We had a lot of problems in Kyogle so we moved to a place called Bowral which is about two hours' drive south of the capital city, Sydney. It was the best thing that ever happened to me because it was there I heard about something that changed my life completely. Someone gave me a small booklet called *Four Things God Wants You to Know*.

'I'd never heard about Jesus before but after reading this little tract, life seemed to make sense to me. I heard for the first time about something called *"sin"*, which is going against God's ways and includes all the bad things we say and do, and that there is a penalty for sin. I needed someone to save me because I couldn't save myself.

'God sent His only son, Jesus, to be my Saviour. He died in my place for my sin and because of his sacrifice on a cross it was possible to receive forgiveness and have what is called "eternal life" when I die. I knew there was something missing in my life. Everything seemed so dull and difficult and I began to wonder if this was all there'd be forever.

'When I read that life was meant to have meaning and be full of hope it really got me thinking. Something in my heart stirred and by the time I'd finished reading that booklet I knew I had the answer to why I was put on this earth. I accepted a different kind of challenge; the most important challenge anyone will ever face in their lifetime. I had to decide whether I believed this message was true and if I did believe it, what was I going to do about it?

'At the end of the booklet, there were some Bible verses to tell me what the next step was. After reading the verses, I prayed a prayer like this, "Lord Jesus, I know I am a sinner and ask you to forgive me for my sin. Thank you for dying for me. I give my life to you so that you will be in control. Thank you for giving me eternal life." This is what we call the gospel—good news. This is the reason we came here to Ninia, to share the good news with the Yali people.'

As I digested this information, a high-pitched wailing began outside and Dad stood up and strode out of the room with my brother and myself in hot pursuit.

Chapter 5
PAT

Mum was standing outside near the washhouse with a weeping woman. It was not the sight of her wailing which alarmed me; that was common. What my eyes focused on was the blood running down her face.

The two women stood together in solidarity. Mum, dainty and delicate, her hair styled in a neat chignon. Her skirt and top although mismatched, fitted her slim build. The barefooted Yali lady, in contrast, wore only her grass skirt, a net bag on her head and mum's loving arm across her shoulders.

Pat consoling Yali lady

'*Nehe*', ('friend') Mum murmured soothingly.

It had happened again. Someone had died and another part of the body was sacrificed.

As mum led the woman to our back door, Dad went to get the medical kit. I followed him. 'Why do people cut off the top of their ears?'

'Remember how I told you there are many different cultures in the world and what we do can often be different from what other people may do? Well, this is one of those times. We don't cut off part of our ears when someone we love dies but the people here do. The Dani people even cut off the top of their fingers. It's their way of showing their grief. It's one of their important customs.'

That's horrible! I thought with a shudder.

After attending to the woman, my mum walked slowly back inside but not to the classroom, rather, to sit by the cast iron stove. Dad lifted the blackened kettle which spent its life patiently simmering.

'A cup of tea?'

'Thanks, love, that would be good.'

'It's a difficult concept to understand, let alone accept, isn't it?' he said as he gave her a quick hug. She looked like she was lost in her thoughts and didn't answer him.

It had taken a long time before the women would come anywhere near us. 'They all seem very scared, Stan,' mum would say.

'I imagine their fear stems from the fact this is a male-dominated culture, dear. The men are warriors and masters of their own destiny. Their women folk seem to serve the purpose of childbearing, tending the gardens, looking after the pigs and getting the fire wood.'

Yali warriors doing a war dance

'Well, I'm going to persevere until they feel comfortable enough to come to me for any reason. I want them to know that they have value and God has a plan for them too, and not just for the menfolk here,' replied mum.

True to her word, mum would try and buy sweet potatoes from the women by walking to a hill and calling out, 'Siburu! Siburu!'

One day an elderly Yali lady ventured close to our house with her string bag of potatoes. The old lady laid her bag on the ground and with a hesitant smile, pointed at the bag, 'siburu'. Mum was delighted, and nodded and smiled in return. She went to get a container of salt and measured a generous scoop into a large leaf. There was no such thing as money, so the people were paid with shells or salt which they greatly enjoyed.

Nisingga with Yali women

Paying with salt

When the women realised that we weren't dangerous to them more started coming for a 'meet and greet' and soon they wanted to be taken through the house on conducted tours! *'Wa, wa, wa,'* they would chant as they held on to mum's hands letting go occasionally to pinch my brother's and my small cheeks.

Soon Mum was given a new name, *Nisingga*, a term of respect which means, 'our mother'. She was no longer exclusively ours! Both the Ninia Yali and our family were starting to share lives in more ways than one.

Yali women and children

The sound of someone clearing their throat caused us to look over at the door and Arelek's serious face appeared, looking more concerned than usual. He conveyed the message that his wife, Latouwen, was struggling in childbirth and was calling for *Nisingga*.

Mum hurriedly drank the last of her tea and stood up. 'I'll get my medical bag.'

'May I come too, Mum?'

'Yes, Joy, but not for long.'

Both Rod and I sensed that the rest of the day's lessons would be suspended. Mum would be helping Latouwen deliver her baby and Dad already said he was meeting a local man to review some translation work. Rod was keen to check one of his hens who had turned broody refusing to leave the nest. He'd also been waiting for an opportunity to string the new bow he'd made.

Mum picked up a bag containing the items she might need—morphine, scissors, sutures, needles, iodine, her thermometer, stethoscope. She grabbed a frayed baby's blanket from the rough wooden shelf in our kitchen and we both walked quickly across the dirt airstrip and into the small village of huts on the other side.

As we neared the place where Latouwen lived, loud moans could be heard. On reaching the thatched hut, Mum bent down to the low entry doorway and waited for her eyes to adjust to the smoky interior. 'Latouwen, *An let habik wahi.*' ('I've come to help you.')

I couldn't hear the Yali woman's reply but Mum turned to me and said, 'I think it's better if you go back home, as I could be here for quite some time.'

Feeling disappointed, I kicked aimlessly at several small stones lying nearby and gazed around the now deserted village. The women and children were away tending their sweet potato gardens on the mountainsides and the men folk had also disappeared, most likely tending their important pigs and making arrows for future use. I wandered back across the strip.

Hours passed before Mum returned to our house. She looked tired and sad and didn't stop to talk but headed straight for her bedroom.

Bingguok, one of our house help boys, had been keeping Rod and me entertained by making simple music on his *binggong* (jew's harp). He placed a small piece of a reed stem in his mouth which had a thin strip of vine attached to it, then using one hand he tweaked the vine producing a melodic twanging sound. Frowning in concentration, he played his instrument and we smiled at him in encouragement. Rod waited patiently before pleading, 'Can I *please* have a turn, Bingguok?'

Mum came into the room and our attention switched to her. 'Did Latouwen have a boy or a girl?'

'What's the baby's name?'

'When can we go see it?'

Mum looked sad and directed her conversation to Dad, who by now had joined us inside. 'I wasn't able to save the baby but Latouwen will be all right if she rests for now and doesn't go back to work in the gardens straightaway. It's such a sad loss for her.'

As Mum's sobs took over and her shoulders started to shake, Dad stroked her hair comfortingly until her tears subsided.

'It brought back memories of losing our David.'

Dad nodded thoughtfully. Rod and I were puzzled. 'Who was David?' Rod asked.

'You had another brother,' said Dad. 'He was our first baby but got very sick and died when he was only one month old.'

Mum interrupted and said, 'It was a long time ago. I couldn't understand why God let him die. I thought I owned the world with a fence around it when I found out I was having a child.'

'That's sad,' Rod remarked in a quiet voice.

Mum turned to Dad. 'I think I now know why we lost David. Going through that experience has given me the ability to understand and care for Latouwen and the other Yali women. When I told Latouwen earlier about my own baby dying, she looked at me and said, 'Nisingga, *hat holukdeg.*' ('Mother, you understand.')

Dad gently patted Mum's back. 'Children, did I ever tell you how I met your Mother?'

'No!'

'Soon after the Second World War ended, I travelled to Tasmania where I'd been invited to give Bible talks in some churches there. At one of those churches, I noticed a beautiful young lady …'

Mum smiled and I started to giggle.

'And,' continued Dad, 'I deliberately sat opposite her so I could use the one-hour luncheon for intensive study!'

'What did *you* do, Mum?'

'Well, your dad asked me if I'd like to go for a walk with him and I did. We discovered that we thought the same way about many things. Dad was leaving to go to PNG to be a missionary and I wanted to go to Bible College after I finished my nurses' training. We had to wait four years before we married and one year after that little David was born.'

One night several months later I woke up feeling afraid. The moon was highlighting the scary shadow of the swaying pandanus tree outside. As I hid my head under the blanket I couldn't shake the unnerving feeling that someone or something was trying to watch me through my bedroom window.

I hopped out of bed to tell Mum about my fear and to ask whether I could sleep in my parents' room. A light from the kerosene lamp shone at the other end of the house and I headed for it like a moth. Mum was sitting at the dining table wiping tears from her eyes.

'What's the matter?'

'Oh, I'm thinking about Wesley and Hilary and wondering how they are getting on since they moved to Melbourne from Tasmania to attend High school. I miss them so much.'

I crawled into her lap. 'When will we see them again?'

She sighed. 'I don't know. Maybe there could be a way for them to come to Ninia for a holiday next summer. We'll see.'

It felt both strange and sad to me to have brothers and know we couldn't share a life together. Missionaries make many personal sacrifices but splitting up their families would have to be the biggest and most difficult one they make.

Within a year after Wes and Hil had gone back to Australia,

Mum was blessed with another child. This event was to become the highlight of my young life. I was overcome with excitement! As much as I loved my brothers, I desperately hoped for a sister to share my dolls and tea parties with.

When the time came for the birth, Mum, Dad, Rod and I flew back to Karubaga so Mum could have the baby in the small mission hospital there. As soon as I was given the 'okay' to meet baby Janet—'yippee, a girl!' I marched into the birthing room and demanded loudly, 'Where's my baby?!' It didn't bother me that she was only a few hours old. I was ready to set the table for our tea party. There was no understanding on my part that I'd soon be sharing my adorable sister with dozens of Yali people all eager to hold her and affectionately pinch her little cheeks.

Baby Janet with Yali people

Chapter 6

EVERYDAY LIFE

T he day had rapidly lost its heat and the air was getting colder by the minute as I wandered over to our backyard airstrip looking for Rod. Darkness would soon settle in for the night and Mum had asked me to go and tell him it was time to come inside.

'Rodney!'

Rod with bow and arrow

My brother was two years older than me and he couldn't think of anything better than being outdoors tending our chooks, ducks, rabbits and goats.

I called to him a second time but he was focused on shooting arrows into the air. He had been given a bow and some arrows from Luliap, one of his Yali friends, and spent as much time as he could practising the technique—pulling the bamboo string back until it was touching his nose, looking down at the arrow with one eye, lining up a target. He then raised and drew his bow, easing his fingers back off the string and '*whoosh*', released the arrow.

It flew straight up into the air and landed metres away, laying flat on the ground. He tried again with a second arrow and his aim was better, as this one became embedded in the earth.

The Yali designed a variety of arrowheads as Luliap told Rod, 'Some arrowheads called m*inggin* have a long sharpened piece of bamboo to kill the pigs quickly. We shoot birds with a three or four pronged arrowhead called *so'ap* and the ones with the barbs notched into the sides are called *dok* making it difficult to pull out once they hit a person. The bow is made from the wood of a mountain tree called *suon*.'

'Rodney, you've got to come in!'

He turned with a resigned sigh, and with the arrows in one hand and his bow in the other, headed to our house.

Our old house—grass hut with a dirt floor

Our new house—vegetable garden in front

EVERYDAY LIFE

Inside, our little sister Janet was happily playing in a large iron tub half-filled with warm water which had been heated on the wood stove. I threw off my dirty crumpled dress and hopped in with her. Rod had come inside with some corn cobs from our garden. He stripped off to get into the tub as Janet and I got out of the brown water. It was a big effort to get water from the river so we all shared the same bath water. Too bad for the last person having a bath as they came out as dirty as they went in!

Mum was working on dinner. I saw her open a tin of bully beef and my heart sank. I hated the greasy, salty tasting bully beef, the smell of which made me feel sick but there'd be no point in complaining. We ate what was available from the supplies that were flown in from time to time, including bulk bags of flour and powdered milk.

The produce from the large vegetable garden Dad planted supplemented our canned diet. Sometimes we bought a leaf vegetable, *wiye*, from the native people. My favourite food was the sweet potato, *siburu*, which the locals ate. It was their main source of food and I felt envious that my friends, Hondoen and Otto, would be sitting in their hut eating a delicious ash-encrusted potato.

Janet tugged at Mum's skirt and asked her favourite question, 'havin' puddin' today, Ma?'

'Yes, my darling. We're going to have rice pudding.' She smiled at the happy look on her sweet little girl's face.

After dinner, we had our regular 'family time' together.

'Tonight I'm going to teach you a poem. It's by Robert Louis Stevenson.'

'Isn't he the man who wrote *Treasure Island*?' I asked.

'The very same,' replied Dad. 'But this is a poem he wrote called *The Swing*.

'How do you like to go up in a swing,
Up in the air so blue?
Oh, I do think it the pleasantest thing
Ever a child can do!
'Up in the air and over the wall,
'Till I can see so wide
Rivers and trees and cattle and all
Over the countryside—
'Till I look down on the garden green
Down on the roof so brown—
Up in the air I go flying again,
Up in the air and down!'

Our own swing

'Off to bed now children, we've got a big day tomorrow.' Mum was referring to 'clinic day' where she would treat the Yali for their sores and injuries, as well as give the people immunisations.

Pat and Joy on clinic day

Baby health clinic

Malnourished child

Every day many tasks needed to be done. There were no malls or markets, no electricity or running water, no washing machine or dishwasher. Water had be collected from some distance away and then carried to our house in large tins.

Carrying water

Some of the older *elahaki omalik* (boys)—Bingguok, Yeikwaroho, Luliap, Erariek and Foliek, became our family's closest companions. They helped us in and around the home and took loving care of Rod, Janet and me. We trusted them completely.

One rainy day Foliek went to pick some vegetables from our garden and I was keen to help. 'Wait for me, Foliek!' I called out, but he was long gone. Eager to catch up to him, I ran as fast as I could in the drizzling rain but as I crossed a small wooden bridge, I slipped and gashed my thigh on the jagged edge. My screams alerted Foliek, who abandoned his plan to get vegetables and raced back to my side. Concerned to witness my sobs and the large volume of blood, Foliek quickly lifted me up and carefully carried me back to Mum so she could patch me up.

Rod with his Yali friends

Many funny things can happen when two different cultures come together. 'Have you children seen the potty I left outside?'

'Yeah, I think I saw a man wearing it on his head this morning, Mum.'

Mum's jaw dropped before her laughter bubbled up. 'Okay, a hat with a handle. Who would have thought?'

It soon became apparent that anything left outside was considered public property.

A potty hat

A recycled comb

EVERYDAY LIFE

Dad continued with the task of trying to learn the Yali language. He wrote down as many words and phrases as he could. Learning their language was a bit like playing charades. He would act out everything to find out what a word was and then he'd have to write down the sound of the word.

One of the men who helped him in this translation work during the early days at Ninia was a man named Suwe.

Dad, me and Suwe

At first, Suwe seemed to think it rather comical, this strange *duong* (man) providing such entertainment and hid his toothy smile behind his hand.

'I'm not giving up on this,' Dad would say with determination, and day after day, Suwe would be subjected to the humorous actions of the mad white man.

It was all too easy to make mistakes with translations, as my parents had discovered when they were missionaries across the border in PNG. Once my grandma from Tasmania had sent my older brother Wes a toy rabbit and Mum told one of the Papuan boys that the rabbit was a gift from Wes' grandma. Later Mum overheard the boy telling his wide-eyed friend the dead rabbit *was* Wesley's grandma!

Mum was keen to help the Yali women learn to read and write. Of course she wasn't going to impose learning English on them. They were Yali and had their own language, which had never been written down.

'Joy, I want you to help me tomorrow. I am going to put the Yali ladies who have shown an interest in learning to read into two groups. I'll take one group and you can take the other.'

It didn't occur to me that I was too young for such a task. What had to be done was done in my family, so I became a teacher to a group of Yali women and girls. They had never before seen paper or anything written. It must have been puzzling for them to have a small white girl instruct them to sit down and say, 'look at the paper and listen to me when I point to this mark.' Dad had made a list of basic words to sound out for the women and girls. 'Soyee, you can look after my baby if I am to look at these strange white leaves.' Hmm, no one said it would be an easy job!

Mum with her reading group

My students AND a baby on my back!

Joyful noises filled the air making me feel happy. The local people were preparing a rare feast because they were going to honour some important guests from another area.

Feast preparation

Cooking lesson

Luliap explained the preparation process to me. 'First, we need to find large rocks and heat them for a long time. We dig big holes in the ground. The women will go and collect all the greens like *yerimingga*, *suet*, *wiye* and *kol* from their gardens.'

'What about the siburu?' 'Yu'o, Soyee, you can have your favourite food, it will be cooked in with everything else! The men will slaughter the pigs and remove the insides. Would you like to have one of the pig's bladders to play with later?'

'O … kay. What do I do with it?'

'The urine will be emptied from the bladder and it will be filled with *'basso'* (a fern), as well as other leaves and bits of meat. We tie the bladder off and you can throw the bladder to the other children across the pit. After that we put the bladders into the pit to cook with the rest of the food and then they will be eaten.'

I ran off to find Hondoen to remind her about the bladder game and it wasn't long before I located her and some of the other children a short distance away near their village. They were sitting

EVERYDAY LIFE

in a small circle engrossed in one of their favourite pastimes—taking turns to check the tight curls on one another's heads for a delicacy called '*fi*'. Another name for them is 'head lice'. My friends looked up momentarily and greeted me with wide smiles. I hastily joined them on the ground and watched as nimble fingers parted each section of the thick curly hair and thumbnails connected with a small parasite. As quickly as possible, the luckless nit would be transferred to someone's mouth. Yum! I was keen to get my fine straight hair checked as well and could never understand why the others thought it such a source of merriment that I would do so. Not that my head ever seemed to be as productive, much to my mother's relief!

We were all eager for the feast to be ready but decided to go for a walk to pass the time. The others took their *ilit* (rain cape made from pandanus leaves) with them. 'The rain will come,' one of them declared.

Heavy rain had held off for most of the day but the occasional drizzle kept the long grass wet. I picked up a useful-looking stick and slashed aimlessly at the vegetation as we walked further from the village until suddenly Hondoen grabbed the stick from my hand and started using it herself.

I stopped and asked for it back.

'*Nerim*,' she said, meaning 'don't want to.'

I felt my anger rising. Although we were presumably similar ages (it was difficult to know for certain as the Yali didn't celebrate birthdays), I was taller and slightly larger than her. I felt a sudden urge to push her, which I did, but unfortunately, she wasn't prepared for such an assault and went tumbling into the long grass. The surprise attack from the normally placid white girl caused a wail to go up and it became louder and longer!

'I'm sorry, Hondoen!' but she had already started to run back to her village. Hondoen was of course, the daughter of Dongla, the village chief! *Oh, no,* I thought, *Dongla will see his daughter's tear-stained face, and after she told him how I behaved, he will come after me and chop my head off.* I was so terrified that I bolted for my home to hide.

After what seemed like a long time of squeezing my body in behind a cupboard, common sense prevailed. *Dongla will have more important things to do than to hunt me down,* I thought. I went outside and eventually spotted Hondoen laughing and chatting with the other children and my fear vanished. She waved me over and I sat down beside her, glad to be friends again.

Joy and friends

'*Do to others as you would have them do to you.*'
Luke 6:31

Chapter 7

THE BREAKTHROUGH

Progress with sharing the message about Jesus with the Yali, was slow for a number of years after our arrival in Ninia, but one day a group of Yali came and consented to sit down and listen to the Word of God. Dad held a daily Gospel service which reached a peak of about 250 people on a weekday and around 400 people on a Sunday.

'It's very encouraging to see how many people want to come,' remarked Dad. 'I believe we will soon have a strong Christian community here in Ninia.'

It wasn't long though before many of the men and women, their curiosity satisfied, stopped coming; others sidled confidentially up to Dad and said, 'We have been coming for a good while now and listening to your words. When are you going to pay us for listening?'

Dad however persevered and constantly looked for ways to illustrate from the Yali culture the truths of the Christian faith. 'Bingguok, why do the Yali fear snakes so much?' Dad was also curious about the reason the Yali smeared themselves with mud. Bingguok scratched his head for a moment as if wondering how to get the Yali message over to this determined man standing in front of him. 'A very long time ago, a snake challenged a bird to a race. The bird flew very quickly to the finishing place but the snake, of course, was a lot slower and when it had finally got to the end it slithered up to the bird and mocked him by saying, '*Fong, fong, fong, fong.*' (mud on you, mud on you). Ever since, the Yali have smeared mud on their bodies as a sign of mourning. If the snake had won the race, all the men would have eternal life because when a snake sheds its skin, it rises to renewed life and becomes immortal.'

'That's very interesting, Bingguok!' Now I can explain the Bible's account of the snake and how sin came into this world. Do you have any more beliefs like this one you could tell me about?'

'When we see the band of colour in the sky, we believe the red band means "blood" and we ask, "who has died?"'

Dad was very pleased. 'How wonderful!' I will use this illustration to explain to the Yali people that God sent his own son, Jesus, down from heaven, to shed his blood for mankind. He put his bow in the sky (a bow with no string), as a sign of His mercy to those who trust Him. He would make an eternal agreement between himself and them.'

Stan's diaries:

> Unseen by us the Word of God took root in some hearts and sprung up into eternal life. One day I went with some young men to visit the villages on the other side of the Heluk River. Halfway across the river we got into a deeper channel and with two young men in front of me, I was swept down the torrent. Though burdened with a pack I swam to the bank, seeing as I did so, the lads being carried helplessly along with the surging water that swept like waves over the boulders in the rapids. One boy, his face covered with blood where he smashed against the rocks, was borne into a backwater and pulled ashore by his friends. I raced over the rocks to where the other lad was clinging, winded, to a boulder in the torrent and got him ashore. 'Arelek', I asked him, as we climbed the mountain to the villages above us, 'where would you have gone if you had died in the river just now?' 'I would have gone to heaven, he replied confidently, 'I prayed to God to save me when I was in the river.'

'Pat, this is the breakthrough we've been praying and longing for. There seems to be a deepening understanding of the truths preached,' said Dad.

The Yali people in the upper Heluk Valley began to show a greater interest in the message my parents had come to share with them.

'Hurry up children, we want to commence our walk soon.' Dad was a stickler for being organised and always had a plan. The whole family sometimes went together on one of Dad's missions.

Today we were heading to the large village at the other end of our valley where we stayed in a tent and the villagers would crowd around curiously all day. Dad would exclaim, 'It's like living in a fishbowl, isn't it?'

Bruno de Leeuw (or Uncle Bruno as we children called him) was also based in Ninia for the first couple of years with the Yali. His own small, thatched roof house had been built on a rise near the bottom section of the airstrip. He was often away trekking to villages some distance from Ninia. Occasionally he and Dad would trek together. One such time the two men planned a week long trek further into the eastern valleys. 'We would need a number of men to accompany us Bruno, to help carry the supplies. I'll ask around to see who'd be willing to go with us.'

Bruno de Leeuw

'Stan,' Mum called out, 'there's a man outside the front of the house. He insists on speaking with you.'

Dad put down his pen and stretched, pushing back his chair.

'Better see what this is about then.' He walked outside and as he came around the corner of our home, noticed an old man patiently squatting on the ground. 'Nare,' Dad greeted the man who was looking at him intently.

'My name is Amalek and I hear that my son, Arelek, has said he'll go with you to the eastern valleys.'

Amalek

'Yes, that's true.'

'He must not go. No one should go. The people there are cannibals and they will kill and eat you!'

'Well, Amalek, I am not fearful of them because the God I serve will look after us and won't let anything happen that isn't a part of his plan.'

'What did he say in reply to that, dear?' asked Mum later.

'He spat, grunted contemptuously and muttered something that I couldn't hear. It was probably a scathing comment on the stupidity of all white men!'

Undeterred Dad and Uncle Bruno, together with Arelek and three Dani men, who had come to help carry supplies, left for the distant valleys in the east.

Stan's diaries:

> The first day we clambered over the rocky edges of the deep gorge through which the Heluk River flows. Each day following, either led us over a high rain-soaked mountain where we stumbled through a labyrinth of moss-draped trees and twisted roots, or down spine-jarring precipitous ridges, over roaring mountain torrents and up again with labouring lungs to the top of the next ridge.
>
> We entered each new valley warily, for we knew nothing of the people there, but in each place, we received an exuberant, if somewhat nervous welcome. Hundreds of men lined the ridges above us, yodelling the news of our coming, while scores followed us along the track. We told these men to leave their bows and arrows by the side of the track and follow us unarmed and we were relieved when they did.
>
> At one place called Bangga, a crowd of men were seated at the top of a ridge. We climbed up to them and held out our hands to take their wrists in the customary greeting, but we found out later that their way of greeting was to hold out the hand palm

upwards and make little beckoning gestures with the fingertips. Consequently, when we approached them the front ranks hurriedly stood up and retreated, trampling the rear ranks underfoot as they did so. I learned from this experience to be careful in my assumptions of how one is greeted!

One day we walked some miles up a swift stream and then almost vertically up a mountainside, walking in an eerie silence through the fog-shrouded dripping forest. After seven hours we came down off the mountain into the sunshine again and saw before us the great mountain walls guarding the farther valleys, which were our ultimate objective.

Here there was a tiny village perched on a razor-back ridge that plunged awesomely to a turbulent river roaring through a gorge thousands of feet below. At this place, we were getting into a new language area and the people seemed apprehensive, so I took out my harmonica and commenced playing it. They listened intently, but whether it was with enraptured enjoyment or in stunned silence I could not tell! After that I entertained them by taking out my false teeth, and as Bruno wore glasses they probably thought we were most unusual beings, whom it would be safer to leave alone.

Seng Valley Yali

> For another half a day we struggled on toward the gateway of the next valley, where an aerial survey had revealed an airstrip site, but then we had to turn back. Our food was running low, our men were exhausted and frightened and it was unwise to proceed any further. We returned over the long weary way we had come. Footsore and tired, but with a haunting vision of those unreached stone-age people in their time-forgotten valleys.

Not long after returning to Ninia, Dad asked the village chief, 'Dongla, how about we build a large shelter which could serve as a school or church for when it is raining?'

Dongla looked at Dad as if the *duong* (man) had lost his mind.

'No, we'd rather squat or sit outside in case any of our enemies from other villages appear,' he replied. 'We will have our bows and arrows ready and take a good aim.'

Dad came inside to tell Mum he decided not to worry about the building, 'It's better that the people feel free to come and if it means holding church in the open air then that's fine with me.'

Church service at Ninia

After Arelek's conversion to the Christian faith, a small group of Yalis came to the realisation that they too, wanted to know and follow this man, Jesus, who lived, died and was resurrected and had the power to transform lives from endless fear and pain to one of hope and peace.

'Tonight at the service I'm going to challenge the Christians to get rid of any fetishes they still cling to.' Dad had been concerned about this matter for some time. 'No-one can wholly follow the Lord while they still have fetishes, just as he cannot be really the Lord's, while he still had idols.'

'What exactly is a fetish, Dad?' asked Rod.

'They're things that the Yali think of as having magical powers.

They might be flat stones, moulded balls of fire-baked clay, lumps of desiccated pig fat from pigs sacrificed to evil spirits, or arrows that have killed or wounded people.'

'That must be why Luliap got cross with me one day. I tried to find him and when I couldn't I went to his hut and looked in. On the wall of his yogwa there was something strange hanging and I wondered what it was, so I went in to have a look, then I heard Luliap's voice behind me, "Soyee, don't touch that!" I told him I was sorry and didn't know what it was. He said, "No, you must not know. Now go back to your home."'

Mum glanced up from her sewing, 'Firstly, Joy, you can't wander into someone's yogwa when you feel like it. It's disrespectful and yes, it may have been a fetish of some kind.'

As planned, Dad spoke to the small group of Christians and taught them what the Bible says about idols. 'In the book of Isaiah, we are told that idols are powerless—they know nothing, they understand nothing, they cannot save anyone. Yet you are still holding on to your idols—your fetishes! You are not totally trusting God to save you and help you. You cannot follow both God and your lifeless fetishes.'

The men became silent at this revelation until suddenly Dongla jumped up and announced, 'I'll burn mine tomorrow!'

The next day more of the Christians at Ninia decided that they too, would destroy their fetishes.

Stan's diaries:

> Suddenly like a leaping flame the idea spread among the Christians. Yodelling and whooping, they went racing up the mountain to their villages, dived into the men's club-houses and started dragging out of

their dark corners the bags of fetishes. They carried them down to the airstrip (the most central place) to be burnt. Even the old die-hard makers of magic spells surrendered theirs for destruction. For two or three hours the eager group of young men ran from village to village, bringing great heaps of filthy, smoke-blackened net bags and heaping them up ready for burning.'

Fetish burning

Not long after the people of Ninia burnt their fetishes, other Yali people in nearby villages decided they too, would like to burn their fetishes. One of these villages was called *Liligan*, a short distance from Ninia. Dad, in his desire to encourage the new Christians there, went over to the village and taught from the

Bible. The people of Liligan told him, 'We know of others who live in the lower part of the Heluk Valley and want to hear more about this "new way", will you go and teach them?'

There was no reason to believe that this wasn't true and at the next prayer meeting held at Ninia, Dad stood up and announced, 'We have had a request from people in the lower Heluk to go and preach the gospel of Jesus to them. Is there anyone here who is willing to go?' Two young Yali men, Yeikwaroho and Bingguok, who had become like part of our family and who were also among the first to become Christians at Ninia, got to their feet. 'Yo, nit laul.' ('Yes, we will go')

Yeikwaroho and Bingguok planned to set off the following morning, on 11th June 1966, with a large coloured chart illustrating the 'broad and narrow' way, which Dad had made for them, but with preparations taking longer than expected the day was slipping away.

'My friends,' said Dad, 'it will be getting dark before you get all the way there, so I suggest you sleep at the first village and not go further today.'

The two young men set off confidently but unbeknown to us at the time, had ignored Dad's warning.

As dusk fell the sound of wailing could be heard in the distance. Within minutes the wailing got louder and Mum saw a couple of women near the airstrip crying and beating their chests. She walked over to them and asked, 'what's the matter?' 'Yeikwaroho and Bingguok have been killed!' came the unbelievable reply.

'No, it can't be true!' We stood near our house trying to make sense of the terrible news. A Yali man standing near us pointed to the smoke from a fire in the distance and said, 'See? That is where Yeikwaroho is being eaten.'

Rod fainted. Mum attended to him while I held Janet's hand

and stood silently, shocked by the news and not knowing what to do. Dad had gone over to speak with the growing crowd who were gathering nearby.

By this stage, it was too late in the evening to get help from anywhere else. Dad did what he could to reassure the local Ninia people. They were expecting the murders to be followed up by an attack on their villages. We spent an almost sleepless night numbed with shock and grief, for the two young men had been so close to our family.

Early in the morning Dad contacted MAF and asked that police be brought in immediately. Within an hour the town of Wamena, in the Baliem Valley, sent in a district officer and four policemen. Dad briefed them about the recent events and asked them to go with him to investigate the scene of the murders in order to find out exactly what had happened to Bingguok and Yeikwaroho. As Dad, together with Luliap, the policemen, and several young local Yali men walked out of Ninia, they were repeatedly warned of the potential danger by other Yali. Nevertheless, the men continued, and the women along the track wailed even louder.

'The Lord is with me; I will not be afraid.
What can man do to me?
The Lord is with me; he is my helper.
I will look in triumph on my enemies.'

Psalm 118: 6,7

Chapter 8

SHOOT TO KILL

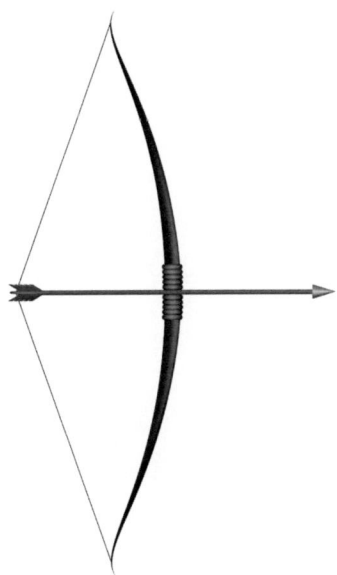

'It's getting late. I think you children need to go to bed now. There's no point in waiting up to see Dad. They probably decided to stay overnight and will be home in the morning.' Mum prayed again for safety for Dad and the other men, then came and tucked Rod and me into our beds before checking on little Janet who was already fast asleep.

My eyelids grew heavy and the events of the day dimmed as sleep overtook me...

Suddenly I was finding it hard to breathe. My heart was pounding as I ran out of the house quickly with my brother.

We could no longer see where Mum and our little sister were. We just kept running. I could hear the shrieks and yells of the native warriors and the sound kept getting closer.

Never had I known such a feeling of terror, for I knew how sharp the pointy ends of those arrows were, having seen them fly into a pig and bring the hapless animal to its knees in an instant. If one of those arrows entered my body it would mean the end.

My whole body was shaking and my legs felt wobbly. I realised that it was impossible to outrun dozens of wild warriors trying to kill me and my family.

Where was Mum?

Shoot to kill

'Joy, wake up! You need to get dressed as we are going to be flying out of Ninia very shortly. I want you, Rod and Janet to stay inside the house until I come back for you. Do you understand? Dad has been shot by hostile tribesmen and I don't know how bad he is. He's being carried to the airstrip and we need to be ready to leave Ninia.'

I jumped out of bed and found the clothes I'd been wearing the previous day quickly putting them on. Janet wanted to find Mum so I distracted her by helping her put on her shoes while Rod went and looked for his clothes. We tried not to cry over the worrying situation. Rod spoke up, 'I hope he's not badly hurt.'

Mum came rushing back to the house after seeing Dad off on the plane which had been waiting at the top of the airstrip. She was out of breath as she spoke, 'Dad is still alive. The pilot will be back for us as soon as he can.' She began to hurriedly throw clothes and other personal items into a suitcase—enough for a few days.

Within the hour the plane returned and the rest of us were flown to Karubaga. We went straight to the small hospital where we were met by Dr Jack Leng who had only recently arrived from Scotland. Dr Leng updated Mum on Dad's condition, 'he's critically ill, Pat. He has five arrow wounds, lost a lot of blood and is very weak.'

MAF flew from the north with equipment, south with another doctor to assist, east from the town of Wamena with supplies and west with pilot George Boggs, who being the same blood group as Dad, gave his own blood in direct transfusion. Other intravenous fluids were necessary and these had only arrived at the small mission hospital a few days earlier after being on order for nine months!

While mum waited and prayed at the hospital, Rod, Janet and I were looked after by other missionaries nearby. Jessie Williamson, a nurse who had arrived only weeks before from Australia, assisted the two doctors. Nine hours later the exhausted team finished operating on Dad. Nothing more could be done except pray. Hundreds of people, including the local Dani Christians at Karubaga, the Yali Christians in Ninia and missionaries from all over West Irian (DNG), began praying for his healing.

Mum took turns with the other nurses to care for her husband. When Dad finally improved and regained some strength our family flew out to the coast so that he could have further tests and x-rays taken at the government hospital. It would be some months before he would be able to resume his work in Ninia so we got on yet another plane and flew across the border to the country of Papua New Guinea in order for him to rest and recuperate.

Stan's diaries:

> When we reached Liligan we were informed that the enemy were waiting in ambush for us at the Heluk River so we proceeded very cautiously down the forested mountain and through the precipitous gorge that followed. There was no sign of any opposition and we came at last to a flimsy bridge across the river.
>
> At this point, the district officer, who had fallen and grazed his knee, decided to return with his police to Ninia. I knew that it could be extremely dangerous to go on without them, but burdened and broken-hearted over the death of the two young men, I felt that I could not face the Christians at Ninia again without doing all that was in my power to find out what happened to their friends, and mine. I gave strict instructions to the Ninia boys who had accompanied us to return with the police and then walked on alone.

At first I walked slowly, carefully investigating the track in front of me before proceeding, for every bush could conceal an enemy and every thicket an ambush. Then the Lord gave me the assurance of his protection and I stepped out more briskly. I had almost reached the first village in the areas where the murders had taken place when I looked back and saw two policemen and the four Ninia youths following me in the distance.

Near the village, I discovered where Bingguok had been cremated by some courageous Liligan people, who had daringly come down to the area to give him their equivalent of a decent burial. By now the police and the young men from Ninia had rejoined me. We could find no trace of Yeikwaroho's body so continued up a side valley and searched the area.

There was evidence of a large body of men having been in the area and then on the side of a hill we found the sweet potato beds trampled down where the murderers had exultantly danced their victory dance after killing the two boys.

By this time it was getting late and we decided to camp for the night in an empty hut at the village near where the lads had been killed. We had seen no one, and as a thick fog covered the ridges around about, it seemed possible that the killers had not even seen us enter the area. With the Ninia boys and a policeman searching around and another policeman with me, it seemed safe for me to start preparing a meal.

I had moved away from the fire in the centre of

the hut and was getting something from a pack near the doorway when I felt a violent stab in my right side and saw a five foot arrow [one and a half metres] embedded in me. I snatched it out with one swift, straight pull, hearing as I did so an exclamation of satisfaction from outside. As I scrambled away from the doorway another arrow pierced my right thigh.

Then we could hear movement all around us. We were surrounded and in a death trap, for the enemy could pour arrows into the hut from every direction. Furthermore, the bright fire made us clearly visible to the attackers.

Before I could throw ashes on the fire to try and extinguish it, another arrow hit me in the left thigh, and when I moved around to the other side of the hut two more arrows struck me, one causing a wound on the right forearm and the other penetrating deeply on the left side, piercing my diaphragm and my bowel. I laughed out loud derisively and called to our assailants to run away home.

Then there arose behind the hut the high-pitched notes of the death wail from the war party, as the assailants triumphantly proclaimed that they had killed me. It was indescribably eerie, and as by this time wounds were beginning to trouble me, I thought for a moment that the attackers might be right.

The policeman who was with me, who had already fired a few ineffectual shots, saw a man creeping up on us with a bow and arrow so he pulled the trigger on his rifle and shot him. The other policeman came up at the same time and commenced firing and the attackers fled.

We gathered our belongings and went back down the valley in the deepening darkness, intending to find a safer place to camp. As we did, I began to realise how serious my wounds were. Every step was agony and the air seemed to be wheezing in and out of me uncontrollably. We soon reached the village near the Heluk River where I planned to sleep. The Ninia boys, though, had different ideas.

'No,' they said, *'Nakni nit let hapmin!'* ('We will help you') We must keep walking through the night. Tomorrow you will be too stiff to move.'

The six hours or more that followed were one long nightmare. We walked in total darkness at first, thinking that the enemy might be following us, but later lit a lantern. Even with its light, the way was only faintly illumined and the track was rough. Sometimes we had to wade along the edge of the rushing river, sometimes we clambered over slippery rocks high above it when a slip would have sent us plummeting down into the torrent beneath. Fallen trees and hidden pot holes made the way more hazardous and time and time again I fell.

Every time great waves of pain swept over me, threatening to blot out consciousness.

Twice I gasped, 'Leave me alone, I'm dying.'

'Oh, my father,' replied one boy, 'come on.'

Gently the boys took me by my hands and led me on.

> Then the Lord's own word came to me, 'I shall not die but live and declare the works of the Lord.' And I clung to the promise as to a staff, as we came out of the gloomy gorge and commenced to climb the mountain beyond. It is hard enough to climb in daylight for a man who is strong and well. At night for someone in my condition, it seemed impossible, but God brought me through. Then, at last, we were walking along the mountain top to Liligan, to rest and partial relief from pain.
>
> Early the next morning the local men made me a litter [a stretcher made from branches] and carried me with wonderful gentleness down the steep mountainside and up the farther ridge to Ninia. There the MAF plane was waiting, ready to take me immediately to Karubaga.'

After spending five weeks in PNG, we returned home to Ninia where the people warmly welcomed us back with happy chants 'wa, wa, wa.' One of our 'boys' had lit the fire, swept the house and placed fresh flowers in a vase.

Mum walked over to speak to one of the young men who had been with her husband on that terrible night. 'Luliap, I'd like to give you a gift in thanks for what you did for Stan when he was shot. You and the other men took wonderful care of him. We'll never forget what you did to help him get back to Ninia.' Mum turned to Dad, 'I'll go over and visit Bingguok and Yeikwaroho's wives. I have some gifts to give them.'

'I'm sure they'll appreciate a visit from you at this time,' he replied.

Mum headed off with her gifts of a towel, bush knife, soap and mirror for each of the two young widows.

Later that day, Dad announced that he'd hold a meeting to speak with the local people. Word quickly got around and soon the school house which had recently been built for the local people, was filled to capacity with eager Yali wanting to hear from the seemingly fearless man who had come not only to *share* his life but was willing to *give* his life, for them.

'Friends, much has happened in recent times. Your prayers combined with the mercy of God, brought me back from the dark valley of the shadow of death to light and life and the love of family and friends. But for Bingguok and Yeikwaroho, there was no return. In their love and loyalty, they gave to the last limit of sacrifice all that they had ... themselves... becoming the first two martyrs of the Yali tribe.'

Sobs broke out in the crowded room and Dongla, wiping tears from his eyes, stood to speak, 'My brother, Bingguok, did not die in vain. He knew it would be dangerous to go to the lower Heluk Valley, but his faith in God made him strong. He has given us an example to live by. I want to be strong like my brother!'

The listeners murmured their agreement.

Dad spoke again, 'you may be wondering what happens next. God's word tells us that when we give our lives to him, we are to be baptised. This is an outward sign of our faith in Jesus. The process is simple. You stand or kneel in some water and another Christian lowers you under the water and quickly brings you up from the water. It's nothing to be scared about. It just shows that you've died to your "old" life of sin and are living in your "new" life in Jesus Christ.'

The challenge of baptism was accepted by the Ninia Christians and four months later, eighteen Yali men and women gathered together by the pond at the top of the airstrip in preparation for taking the next step in their Christian faith.

'I can hear the plane coming,' said Dad as we waited for the arrival of missionaries, Phil Masters and Costas Macris. 'I'm glad they can be here to share in the occasion and see for themselves the progress made in the lives of the Yali. Phil was a tremendous help when he came in to assist with the initial building of the airstrip and Costas too when he and his wife Alky, came to Ninia to fill in for us when we were away that time.'

Our visitors were welcomed as they stepped down from the small aircraft. 'Wonderful you could both be here! Isn't it a beautiful day for such an occasion? Come down to the house and we'll have morning tea before we make our way up to the pond.' Dad sounded as proud as a new father as he shouted to be heard over the noise of the departing plane.

I turned to Rod, 'let's hurry so we can get ourselves a good spot to see everything.' My brother and I ran ahead of the adults and found a grassy area overlooking the pond. The men stood for a time discussing who would get into the water and perform the first of the baptisms. Dad removed his shirt revealing not only his muscled arms but the long scars crisscrossing his torso from the arrow wounds he received only six months earlier.

Stan's diaries:

> I waded with Arelek into the deeper water of the pond and as I did so, the scene before me seemed to dim. The crowd of people on the high banks surrounding the pond, the lofty mountains that walled us in, the bright expanse of ridge and river faded away, and I was once more walking the paths of yesterday with the young man before me.

I could see him again, labouring with me day after day on the construction of our airstrip in our first few months in the valley, working in our house a year or two later, listening attentively to the gospel of Christ at the daily meetings.

Once more we were fording the rushing Heluk River together on our way to preach the gospel to the people on the other side, and the swift flood was sweeping us along. My heart constricted again as he was carried away from me, and then I re-lived the sense of relief I felt as I reached him and pulled him ashore.

The vision vanished. 'Arelek, I asked him, do you believe in Jesus Christ the Son of God?' 'I believe,' he answered. 'Have you forsaken the devil and the ways of evil?' 'I have forsaken them,' he replied. 'Then I baptise you in the Name of God the Father, God the Son and God the Holy Spirit.'

First Yali Christians

'Luliap,' I called, and as he came down into the water, his face alight with joy, I reached out my hand and drew him forward, as he had held mine and led me on some months before. The bright scene before me faded out. It was getting dark in the little dusty hut, dark with the approaching shadow of death, as the arrows pierced my body or rattled against the wall beside me. Then once more I was staggering up the gorge, and the cold black river was lapping against my ankles as if it were going to drag me down into its depth and swirl me along with it.

Luliap was holding my hand, and he seemed to be drawing me up from some deep pit. 'Come on, my father,' he was urging me, as I struggled to retain consciousness, 'come on.' My thought came back to the scene before me. 'Luliap,' I said, 'do you believe in Jesus Christ the son of God?'

With Phil and Costas assisting, each of the converts came forward, as the pictures from the past flashed in swift succession on the screen of memory. One by one they passed through the waters of baptism, a brave little band of brothers and sisters in Christ.

The service finished and the day moved to a close. That evening over a hundred people gathered at the prayer meeting, rejoicing over the baptisms, opening their hearts to the Lord in prayer and listening to the Word of God.

Stan Dale and Phil Masters baptising Ninia Christians

Stan Dale and Costas Macris baptising Ninia Christians

Ninia baptisms

After years of slow-going and setbacks, the church at Ninia was finally established. 'I feel though that in some ways, my work is just beginning,' remarked my dad, 'there are many more people to reach in the valleys and mountains beyond ours.'

Chapter 9

GOOD TIMES

My mother was positively beaming and walked around humming softly. There was an air of great anticipation as we counted down the days to when my older brothers would arrive and spend their summer holidays with us.

Wes and Hil had landed out on the coast at Sentani after four days of travelling from Australia. Missionaries in various locations had taken turns to care for the boys over the course of their long journey.

It was a bright sunny day when my brothers flew into Ninia on the 6th December 1967. Dad, Mum, Rod, Jan and I together with many Yali friends had been straining our ears to hear the sound of the single engine plane.

Wes and Hil's visit 1967

'They're here, they're here!' Rod and I jumped up and down. We all walked quickly to the top slope of the airstrip and stood together along the side as Clell Rogers banked the small plane sharply, came close to the sides of the limestone cliffs above the Heluk River and lined up for the final approach. Smoothly and steadily he brought the little craft down, it bounced lightly along the ground momentarily and settled before roaring back to life as it laboured to climb the final steep upslope. We waited for the pilot to swing the plane around in its take-off position and for the turning propeller to slow to a stop. The Yali around us began their rhythmic chanting as we all surged towards the opening doors. Hil and Wes jumped down to the ground and were soon enveloped in hugs from everyone.

Impatiently I asked, 'Did you bring us anything?'

'You'll have to wait and see, won't you.'

Packages and boxes from the cargo hold of the plane were carried down the 'strip' back to our house accompanied by non-stop chatter.

'Yes!' Wes and Hil had most definitely brought all kinds of items with them, including something delightful called 'lollies'.

'These ones are for you, little sister.'

'Ooh, thanks!' I opened the small paper bag he'd handed me. Inside were the most colourful looking shapes. 'What are they?'

'Those ones are called bonbons, they're hard on the outside and are soft and chewy on the inside. These ones...' Hil pointed to some small square black and coloured layers, 'they're called liquorice allsorts and those ones wrapped in paper are chewing gum. You can chew but don't swallow them!'

'What happens if I swallow them?'

'Well, your insides will stick together.' Hil's smile suggested otherwise.

It didn't take me long to gobble up my portion of the sweets and I craved more. High and low I searched until a thought popped into my head—*perhaps I should check under Hil's pillow?* Bingo! There they were, gleaming like jewels in the sun.

As fast as my greedy cheeks could hold them, in they went. The sticky dribble running down my chin was proof of my approval.

Several hours later, I heard Hil yelling out, 'Hey, where are my lollies?'

By process of elimination and my sticky face, the culprit was soon discovered. Did I feel bad? Yes, but I justified my actions.

'You can get lollies anytime you want and I can't!'

'That doesn't mean you can go and take mine! I'm still telling Mum and Dad what you did.'

After I was given 'the talk' about the wrongs of taking something that didn't belong to me, I apologised to my brother, he gave me his gracious 'I forgive you' and in a few days we were both consoled by the fact that it was his 14th birthday and he was paid back by way of gifts and party food.

Hil's 14th Birthday

The special days kept coming and Christmas Day was no exception. Dad held a church service, after which we joined with the Yali in the preparation of their feast and gave them gifts of salt, soap, pencils and books.

Dad preaching

Christmas Celebration

Church service and pig feast

Waiting for food to cook

I tried to wait patiently for our family gift giving. When we were all seated, Dad gave the presents out in an orderly manner.

Christmas 1967

Wes and Hil had brought with them, a camera for Rod, a doll for me, and another doll for Janet. Our eyes lit up and we wore smiles that stretched from ear to ear.

Dad made a comment and my brothers started to laugh.

'What's so funny?' Mum asked.

'I was reminding the boys about a Christmas we had at Karubaga many years ago when I dressed up as Santa Claus, got up in the attic, made a stomping noise and came down through the manhole in the ceiling,' he chuckled.

Mum gave a slight smile. 'Yes, I remember. You gave our house-help girls such a fright they ran away screaming!'

'Well, I did feel bad for scaring them, but you have to admit it was quite a funny scene.'

'Dad dressed up as Santa?' I piped up from across the room.

'You were too young to remember,' Wes said with a knowledgeable look.

That's the trouble with older siblings, I thought, *they always have to be one memory ahead of me.*

The rest of the holidays passed quickly with my brothers building a hut, going on treks and picnics, and renewing friendships with the Yali people from their earlier time at Ninia. We were also getting ready for New Year and a visit from our friends, the Masters family from Korupun. It was common for MKs to call the adult missionaries 'aunt' or 'uncle'. To my thinking, Uncle Phil and Aunt Phyliss were the perfect example of a missionary couple —kind, sincere, gracious and loving. They had four children— Crissie, Curt, Becky and Robbie.

We began to get our house ready for the influx of visitors, including preparing some beds. As we had no extra mattresses or pump-up beds; we had to make our own. Enough dry moss was collected to make the temporary beds that we kids would use for sleeping, and on the 29th December, the Masters family were shuttled in on two separate flights.

The older children, Wes and Hil, Crissie and Curt were getting reacquainted, 'Hey, it's been a long time since we've seen you guys!' I looked shyly at Becky, 'do you want to see our ducklings?'

Mum and Aunt Phyliss hugged each other warmly. 'How nice to see you again, Pat. We've brought some peanuts, potatoes and passionfruit for you all.'

We spent a happy few days with the Masters and saw in the New Year together. After our brief catch up they returned to their mission station at Korupun and we began to prepare ourselves for saying goodbye to Wes and Hil who were returning to Australia.

The happiness of the last few weeks was replaced with long faces. We dressed in our best outfits, stood in the front garden and tried to smile as we got ready for some family photos. Dad put the camera on a tripod, set the timer and ran back to take his place with the rest of us.

None of us knew it would be our last family photo.

Dale family 1968

Wes and Hil lived in a home for missionary kids and attended school in Melbourne, Australia. Although it was a little too far away from my parents for my liking, I was envious of the Masters' kids, who were at boarding school on the coast at Sentani. The stories of life out there sounded fun, with all the good times they had with the other missionary kids.

GOOD TIMES 117

I approached Mum and Dad one day. 'Can I go to school in Sentani?'

'May I, not can I, and no, you may not!'

'But why?'

'Firstly, we are Australians and we want you to be taught the Australian curriculum. Secondly, we don't have the money to send you to a boarding school.'

I didn't fully understand my parents' explanation but realised that there was no point in arguing about it. Later, I learnt that my family lived by faith. This meant we didn't know how much money we would get or where it would come from. Church folk or maybe family from back in Australia would send us a gift of money from time to time. Sometimes we may have received more than we needed for a month and other times we had to go without certain things.

As a result of not being sent away to school, Rod and I had no choice but to go with my parents to the annual week-long missionary conference held at Karubaga. I was never keen on the occasion as I knew that I'd have to attend the children's program. Apart from Rod, the other dozen or so children were several years younger than me which left me feeling embarrassed and out of place. 'Now children, today I'm going to tell you a story about a royal family,' said a lady from another mission group. She had kindly accepted a request to come and run the children's program so the adults from our mission could have their own sessions throughout the day. 'I'm going to teach you all a song that talks about how we are bright gems in our King's crown and then we will have more fun making crowns to wear.' This part sounded pretty good to me.

Trestle tables had already been set up and on them were placed brightly coloured craft paper, glue, scissors, together with shiny stars and sequins. I began to carefully cut out the shape of my crown and was getting ready to glue on some of the pretty decorations when one of the young boys pushed my hand away from the glue bottle and held on to the bottle himself. I stared at him for a moment before trying to reclaim the bottle...'whack', his fist punched my arm and I saw red. *You're not getting away with that, mate!* I gave him a shove...then felt his slap. 'Stop it!' 'give me the glue', I insisted. 'No!' Our hands reached out to battle over the glue bottle. 'Children, that *is* enough!' Our once pleasant teacher looked cross. 'Joy, you go to that corner over there.' I sulked to the far side of the room and stood there scowling at the mean kid for causing me to be put in a situation where my craft making time would be lost.

When the other mums arrived to collect their little darlings, the teacher was quick to place the blame on me for the run-in with the boy. I watched from the corner of my eye as some of the mothers huddled together, gossiping. One of them glared at me and whispered loudly, 'She's too old to be here. Why don't they send her to school at Sentani?'

I pretended not to hear and waited for Mum. Walking with her to the conference building my family were staying in, I complained loudly, 'I don't want to go back there tomorrow!' and told her what had happened. 'Why do adults say mean things?'

'Sadly we do that, dear, because no one is perfect, not even missionaries. Sin lives in us all!'

'She speaks with wisdom,
and faithful instruction is on her tongue.'

Proverbs 31:26

Chapter 10

SAD, BAD NEWS

Dad and Mum were discussing their plans for an upcoming trip. When I heard 'Korupun' mentioned I paid attention to their conversation.

'Ten days seem a long time to leave you and the children alone here in Ninia, darling. Why don't you take a break and stay with Phyliss while Phil and I are gone?'

'That's not a bad idea. I'd like to see firsthand their situation with the Kimyal tribe. Phyliss probably wouldn't mind some company either.'

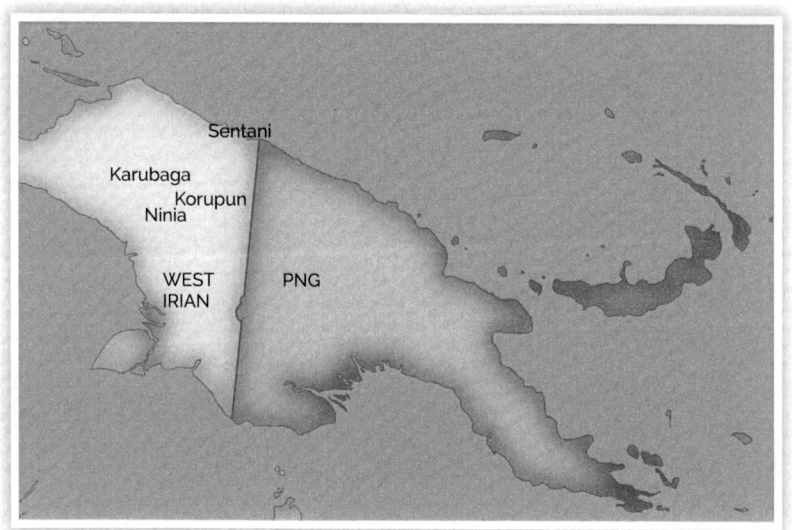

'Hooray!' I was happy with the news that we'd be going to Korupun and even happier that it meant I'd have a holiday from doing school work. 'Why are we going?' I asked Dad. 'Uncle Phil and I plan to go on a trek and make contact with the tribes who live between Korupun and Ninia. We want to share with them the message of God's love. If they seem interested, we'll try and locate a suitable place to build an airstrip.'

Dad's answer seemed reasonable to me.

A week later, Dad, Mum, Rod, Jan, and I, together with a Yali man named Yemu, climbed aboard the Cessna and pilot Clell Rogers flew us to Korupun, a flight of twenty minutes. The tiny settlement was nestled between huge mountains 2,800 to 3,800 metres (nine to twelve thousand feet) high and punctuated with waterfalls.

Korupun

Pilots who flew to Korupun weren't able to see the airstrip until they were on the final approach. They needed to fly close to the mountain cliffs and then turn sharply to start their landing run.

After settling in and enjoying our hosts' warm hospitality, both Dad and Uncle Phil went to check and double check the items they'd need to take with them on the ten-day trek. I bounced up to Dad with my mouth half full of one of Aunt Phyliss's delicious cinnamon rolls. 'I'll miss you, Dad.' 'I'll be back before you know it!' he replied confidently.

The next morning, the rain pounded heavily on the roof. Mum stared out the kitchen window. 'I hope it stops raining soon.'

'We'll wait until lunchtime and then make a decision about whether to leave today,' commented Dad, as he walked over and joined her at the window.

Around midday, the rain eased long enough for the men to commence the long, tiring trek ahead. Before they set off our two families joined hands, prayed for safety and sang the well-known comforting song, 'What a Friend We Have in Jesus'. It was Thursday 19th September 1968.

Three Dani men were also going with our dads, as well as Yemu the Yali, who had come with us from Ninia.

Mum looked worried. 'You've put the radio in, haven't you?'

'Sure have. Expect to get a call from us sometime this evening.'

After a hug and kiss from their spouses, Mum and Aunt Phyliss waved goodbye from the house but we kids followed the men a short distance before my dad turned and said, 'You'd better run back home now.'

Later that night, the radio came to life. 'Korupun ... can you hear me ...?' Uncle Phil's voice crackled from the instrument sitting on a table. 'We have reached the first village safely ... still raining ... will press on in the morning.'

The next day heavy rain set in again at Korupun. There was however, a much bigger concern. There seemed to be something wrong with the Masters' radio. We could receive transmissions but not send out any. 'We won't be able to call for a replacement, Pat. I'll try and see if I can fix it.' Aunt Phyliss went to find a screwdriver and returned to unscrew a part of the radio. She tried the transmitter again. 'No, it doesn't seem to be doing any good. We'll just have to wait until the weather clears and the next plane comes in.'

Two days went by, leaving us with no knowledge of what was happening in the world, including what was happening in the remote area where Dad and Uncle Phil were trekking, as we heard nothing from them. We were truly isolated.

Finally, on the evening of the twenty-second, '… Can you hear us? … We have now crossed the Solo river and expect to enter the Seng valley and arrive in Lugwat tomorrow …'

The two mothers sighed with relief and gave a prayer of thanks for the update.

On the night of the twenty-fourth, Uncle Phil managed to radio a message to us and give a further update on their position. One thing he said puzzled Mum and Aunt Phyliss. The men's plans had been changed. Instead of returning to Korupun as originally planned they were going to keep trekking the longer distance all the way to Ninia. They gave no reason for the change and with the radio transmitter not working at our end, they couldn't be asked about this new plan.

On the twenty-fifth of September, 1968, it rained all night. We listened to a silent radio.

The following day, the sun shone brightly, and as Mum had promised to take Rod for a walk to some waterfalls, they set off with their packed lunch. Aunt Phyliss prepared a picnic for the rest of us close to home in order to hear any further news on the radio.

When Mum and Rod returned from their walk she asked, 'Any news, Phyliss?'

'No. Not yet.'

However, within a short time, static could be heard coming through the small radio and our mums hurried over to listen. '… Anggeruk … here, Karubaga, come… in … I have two Dani men … arrived … news of Stan Dale … and Phil Masters … shot … believed killed … over.'

I watched Mum and Aunt Phyliss as they drew even closer to

the radio, trying to make sense of what was being transmitted. A look of shock passed between them. I didn't want to know anymore so I left the room.

Not long after, Mum came away from the radio to find my brother, sister and me.

'Come over here and sit down, there is something I need to tell you,' she said through her tears. 'A missionary who lives in Anggeruk told Uncle Dave Martin on the radio, that two of the men who went with Dad and Uncle Phil had arrived at Anggeruk, cold and exhausted, and said that the two white men had been shot. It seems that Dad has probably been killed.'

It was difficult to know how long it took for this information to register in my mind and in a way it never really did fully sink in. There was a part of me that thought it wasn't true and tears didn't come, the only thing I managed to say was, 'Can we go home now?' My subconscious mind seemed to be playing tricks on me as the home I referred to was not Ninia, but an unknown Australia.

Sleep didn't come easily to any of us that night but eventually, tiredness overtook Rod, Jan and me. We were not to get much rest however as around 2:00 am a strong earthquake shook the Masters' house and a heavy bookcase toppled over onto Rod's bed, missing him by centimetres. Earlier, Rod and Robbie Masters had been squabbling and when the bookcase fell onto Rod's bed and woke him up, he exclaimed, 'Rob did it! Rob did it!' Our mums dragged the mattresses downstairs where we spent a restless night on the floor, waiting for any aftershocks.

We were to learn later that 'our' earthquake had only been felt in the Ninia, Korupun and Seng areas, as though linking us all together like some kind of a tragic act in a stage play.

MAF, our lifeline, came in the following morning and flew Mum,

Rod, Jan and me back to Ninia. Aunt Phyliss and Robbie were flown out to another, larger mission station where they would be reunited with Crissie, Curt and Becky who were presently away at boarding school.

A search party was put together by other missionaries in West Irian with MAF suspending their usual operations to assist in flying over the area where our dads and the other men had been. One of the Dani carriers who had escaped the attack was flown back from Anggeruk to help locate the killing site. When he managed to get his bearings from the air it became obvious the terrain was too rugged and dense to fly a plane any lower. A helicopter from across the border in PNG was brought in to fly closer to the ground. It landed in our front yard at Ninia, and then made three separate trips to take missionary men Frank Clarke and Jacques Teeuwen, and also the Indonesian policemen who had returned with us to Ninia, to the location of the site.

There was no landing place near the site of the killings so the helicopter pilot hovered low each time in order for the men to jump out. MAF pilot Paul Pontier circled overhead in his small plane for three and a half hours. Mum had to stand by the radio in our home at Ninia and relay the arrival and take-off times of the helicopter to Uncle Paul flying high above, to keep him up-to-date with what was happening on the ground.

Several hours later we heard the *chakk-chakk-chakk-chakk* of the helicopter returning. Frank Clarke jumped out as soon as the landing skids settled on the grassy area in front of our home. Mum walked over to meet him.

'Oh, Pat, I'm so sorry. What we saw was utterly devastating. There were hundreds of bloodied arrows laying everywhere and blood-stained clothing ripped to shreds. All the equipment was trashed, including the radio. There were tell-tale signs of bone fragments. There was no possible way Stan and Phil would have survived such a savage attack.'

Mum held her tears but with shaking hands took some articles from Frank Clarke—Dad's camera and a Bible, which clearly showed the mark of an arrow.

The helicopter pilot, Bob Hamilton from PNG, felt sorry for our loss and in an attempt to cheer us up gave Mum, Rod, Jan and me a ride in his helicopter after which Mum gave him lunch and soon he was on his way back from where he came.

Everyone, it seemed, had their lives to go back to.

The Christians at Ninia were deeply saddened by what had happened but they bravely declared their trust in God. Almost two hundred Yali came to the following Sunday morning service, which was conducted by Luliap.

Soon after, we flew to Karubaga where a memorial service was held a week later.

On that bright sunny day, MAF made fifteen landings by 10:00 am. Around fifty missionaries from all over West Irian came as well as Indonesian officials, local Dani and one of the men who had been on the fateful trek with the two dads and who had managed to make his escape.

The conference building had been beautifully decorated by the missionary ladies of Karubaga. Freshly cut hibiscus and colourful bougainvillea were a part of the floral arrangements on tables and the walls displayed photos of the Seng area where Dad and Uncle Phil had been martyred. A replica of the 'Two ways' chart which my dad had taken on the trek was also on show.

Frank Clarke, an Australian missionary who had arrived in DNG not long after us and who had been part of the recent search party looking for Dad and Uncle Phil, read comforting words from the Bible, 'And we know that in all things God works for the good of those who love him, who have been called according to his purpose; We do not sorrow as those without hope...'

Hymns were sung including one that Mum had chosen, 'Rejoice for a brother deceased, our loss is his infinite gain'. Aunt Phyliss had also chosen a well-known hymn, 'It is well with my soul'.

Myron Bromley from the Christian and Missionary Alliance (CAMA) led the prayer time and prayed God would bring good out of the tragic situation.

American missionary Don Richardson, spoke, 'The first and most natural reaction of the human mind to the martyrdom of a servant of God is always, how strange that God should allow his servants to die in such a manner! The seeming inappropriateness —the paradox—of people who are in the hand of the infinite and almighty God, being made subject to the mere physical violence of the ungodly, is hard for the human mind to resolve.

'We read in 1 Peter 4:12, "Dear friends, do not be surprised at the painful trial you are suffering, as though something strange were happening to you ..." We may well ask, why is it that people who are loyal to Jesus Christ, who endeavour to be as he was, holy, harmless, undefiled—people whose desire it is to live and teach the ethic of heaven itself—why should they be, in every age, the objects of such furious hatred?

> 'There are perhaps, many reasons. I will name what I believe is the main one. The ungodly of this world persecute the body of Christ because they instinctively recognise that body as the vanguard of an invasion from another world, a world diametrically opposed to this one.
>
> 'The ungodly are fighting to hold this planet against that invasion, even though it is an invasion

> by the greatest love and goodness that ever was.
>
> 'Some imaginative men have speculated about the possibility that the world may someday be invaded from outside itself. Little do they realise that an invasion of this world occurred two thousand years ago, an invasion far more subtle, more sophisticated, and far more certain of success than anything that the wildest flight of man's imagination could conceive. The incarnation of Jesus Christ was that invasion.
>
> 'What is God doing [in this situation of the loss of Stan and Phil]? He is turning the temporal pain and physical death of just men into the eternal salvation of unjust men. Is it fair of God to do this? God is able to guarantee their resurrection and there is no soul beyond the reach of God's consolation—as we read in Matthew's gospel, "For whoever wants to save his life will lose it, but whoever loses his life for me will find it."'

I didn't understand or really care what Uncle Don was talking about, so my mind focused on a crack in the rough floor boards near my feet. It was bad enough that my family had all this unwanted attention. All I wanted was to play a carefree game with my friends again.

Pat Dale with Myron and Marj Bromley after the memorial service held in Karubaga

Soon after the memorial service, my family returned to Ninia. The Yali people were waiting for our arrival. Many tears fell and hugs were given and received. It was a sombre time for everyone but Mum tried to be positive as she encouraged the faithful Christians.

She admitted later that she, 'rather foolishly handed out all Dad's clothing to the Yali men, forgetting that they would find no reason *not* to parade around in his shirts and trousers.' Mum, in turn, was encouraged by the fact the little band of Yali Christians grew in their faith and did not, as some of the other missionaries predict, lose courage and vanish into the mountains. Instead, they continued to spread the gospel message of hope and reconciliation and even ventured closer to the areas where the killings had taken place.

A replica of the two way chart Stan Dale used on final trek

For our family, though, the inevitable could no longer be put off. One of the single missionary ladies, Margaret Crawley came to Ninia and helped Mum pack up our things. We left behind most of our bulky items and could only take what would fit in our suitcases.

As Mum stood looking out of the front windows from our home in Ninia one day, she gazed at the mountains in the distance where Dad and Uncle Phil had been martyred and was greatly comforted because there, over the spot where the men would have shed their blood, stretched the most beautiful double rainbow!

Joy and Jan with their Yali friends

When Mum, Rod, Jan and I flew away from Ninia for the last time, it didn't seem real to me that I wouldn't be going back. The place which had been my home for most of my life was fading into the mist and clouds. As I stared sadly out of the small Perspex window of the plane, it began to dawn on me that life as I knew it was now over. Never again would I run across our rough grassy airstrip, which Dad helped build, to the village on the other side, where I would laugh and play with my best friends.

I would no longer taste the sweetness of the *werema* (pandanus nut) in season or enjoy siburu straight from the hot ashes of a fire. How could I leave my 'big brothers', Luliap, Erarick, Aralek and the others? They were my family!

Just before Dad died he had completed the translation of the gospel of Mark for the Yali and Mum now wanted to type up copies for the Indonesian Bible Society and for future translations, so we stayed in Karubaga until she finished this task.

On the final Sunday when we were at Karubaga, a missionary, Dave Martin, was the speaker at the church service. The Bible reading came from Exodus chapter thirty-three. Mum was still grieving and unsure of the future but when verse fourteen was read out, she said it struck her like an arrow; not the kind that killed her husband but the kind that hits with a message that was straight from God himself.

> 'My presence will go with you, and I will give you rest.'

She left that service knowing without a doubt that God was with her.

Pat Dale and Janet, Phyliss Masters and Rob at Karubaga

Aunt Phyliss decided to stay on in West Irian and went back to Karubaga to live with the Dani people. God gave her an extra special gift when her youngest son, Tim, was born about six months after Uncle Phil had been martyred.

'We're going back to Australia now,' Mum told Rod, Jan and me. 'We need to be with Wes and Hil.'

One of Mum's missionary friends had been talking with her after the memorial service, 'What are your plans, Pat?'

'I believe it's time for me to return to Australia permanently and make a home for my children. I feel worn out after all the dramatic events of the past eight years. Many folk don't know that Stan and I were in PNG for a long time before coming here. I'm sure God will raise others up to continue the work amongst the Yali now.'

Not long after this conversation, Mum opened a letter sent from Australia.

'Dear Pat', it read, 'my wife and I would like to offer you the use of a fully furnished house in Melbourne when you return to Australia ...' Mum was speechless at first but then remarked, 'I don't know why we should be surprised at such generosity. God promises to look after His children and in particular widows and the fatherless.'

Our return flight to Australia landed us in Melbourne one hot summer's day of December 1968. There to meet us at the airport were our wonderful grandparents from Tasmania. They took us to a lovely home where we were reunited with Wes and Hil.

'Is this really going to be our house?' Rod and I looked in amazement at the small, neat weatherboard structure surrounded by tall eucalyptus trees and flowering acacia shrubs in the outer eastern Melbourne suburb of, Upwey.

'Yes, for as long as we need it,' replied Mum softly. 'It only has two bedrooms but that won't be a problem. The three of you boys will sleep in one and the girls and I will sleep in the other.'

It took some time for us all to adjust to life in a civilised part of the world. 'I don't want to wear shoes,' complained Rod, 'they're too uncomfortable!'

'Well, you'll just have to get used to them. They won't let you go to school here in bare feet.'

'This sounds tasty for dinner—Beef with vegetables.' Mum held up a can to show the black and white label, put the can on the table and went to find something to open it with.

I picked up the can and turned it over. It said 'pet food only'. 'Er, Mum, you may want to read the rest of the label.'

Taking the can from my hand she took a closer look and frowned. 'Oh dear, I'm still learning about all the products on the supermarket shelves. It's so confusing.' As she went to find something else more suited to the human palate, I tried my hardest NOT to think back to our last canned meal!

One day Mum returned from the mailbox with a wide smile on her face. 'What did you get in the mail?'

'We got another answer to prayer!' she exclaimed. This is the third time lately that someone I don't know has sent me a cheque which is the exact amount needed to pay a bill.'

Six months after moving into the small home in Upwey, we moved again. Mum found out that she was eligible to get a loan from an organisation called 'Legacy' who helped war widows. 'We understand that your husband didn't die in war, Pat, but you can still access our services due to the fact he had been a former soldier,' said the kind looking man from Legacy. With her widow's pension, some part-time night duty work as a nurse and the Legacy loan, Mum bought a larger house for us in the leafy suburb of Ringwood East. We were all pleased to have the extra space especially with three teenage boys in the family. Janet and I would no longer have to share a bed, only a bedroom.

Weeks had their habit of turning into months and gradually life settled into some kind of haphazard routine.

'Joy and Janet, I've been asked to speak at a church on the other side of the city. I haven't been able to find a babysitter for you so you'll need to come with me.'

I groaned. 'Do we have to?'

'Yes, your brothers have their own plans and I can't leave you home alone.'

Mum disliked publicity and how the events of our life in DNG/West Irian, had propelled her into the limelight, but she was asked to do a lot of public speaking and spent many hours preparing talks to give at churches and small groups around the country. Unfortunately, we children often had to go too.

So on a cold winter's evening in Melbourne, we rugged up in coats and warm scarves, Mum started our small Toyota Corona and nervously took to the busy roads. 'I hate driving,' she muttered. Little wonder, after having lived for a long time in a place where there were no roads.

She had the greatest difficulty finding her way around a new area and needed to pull the car over to the side of the road frequently in order to study the map under the dim street lights. It wasn't long before Janet and I drifted off to sleep, leaving Mum with her frustration.

Eventually, I woke up and asked, 'Are we there yet?'

'No. I've been driving around and around for two hours so the meeting will be over by now. We're going home.'

For a long time I imagined that my dad was only lost and one day he'd walk through the front door of our house in Melbourne, saying something like, 'Whew, it took some time but I finally found my way out of those mountains!' My head knew that he was gone, but because there was no body to be found, my heart didn't accept his loss.

One day after moving to our new home in Ringwood East, I learnt more about the horrific details surrounding Dad's death and it was only then I could grieve properly and finally accept the fact he was gone forever.

A strange car had pulled up in the driveway and a well-dressed man and lady got out. Mum greeted them politely and introduced them to us as Mr and Mrs Manning. After a few general questions were asked of us, we kids made our escape from adult conversation.

Some time later, when I heard their car start and the front door close, I found Mum and asked, 'who were those people?'

'They were missionaries in Africa but now they live in Australia and Mrs Manning is a writer. She wants to write a book about the events which happened in DNG and came to talk to me about it.'

'What exactly did happen when Dad and Uncle Phil went to tell that tribe about Jesus?'

Mum looked at me for a moment and then told me to sit down on the lounge next to her. With her arm around my shoulders, she began to fill in some of the details, 'When your dad, Uncle Phil and the native men arrived at a place called Lugwat, which was about thirty kilometres from Korupun, they encountered people who were hostile towards them, so Dad and the others made the decision to move on and camp further away. They decided on a longer and safer, in their minds, route to Ninia. There was a shorter route but it was where Dad had been shot two years earlier, so they decided to follow a river upstream and then climb a higher pass and go that way.

'The following day, they continued walking and finally arrived in the Seng valley, which would lead them to Ninia. Throughout the day, however, they had been stalked by tribesmen from the hostile area, and as they headed north into an area called Wikbun, the hostile tribesmen continued to follow them.

Photo of final trek recovered from Stan Dale's camera.

'On the Wednesday, which was the 25th September, Dad, Uncle Phil, Yemu, together with the three other carriers, woke up after an uneasy night and proceeded to pack up their gear. Danger was all around. Men were watching them closely, armed with bows and arrows. Dad and the others calmly and silently began to walk. The warriors followed. What had begun as a small group of hostile men grew larger in number, as each village along the way joined forces with them. Soon there were hundreds of hostile warriors stalking the men.

'Some of the hostile men, who saw the duongs as a threat, came close to Dad with their bows drawn, arrows at the ready. Dad held up his hands and tried to reason with the men, saying that he wasn't there to hurt them, but there was no understanding by the men.

'Dad knew what was about to happen, and in order for the others to stand a better chance of getting away, he urged them to run. Yemu was reluctant to leave Dad and knew for certain what was going to happen, but he and the other three carriers soon fled. Uncle Phil and Dad were left to face the warriors.

'Yemu and the other men who had been trekking with Dad and Uncle Phil didn't run far away and were watching from a distance. They saw your dad being shot with dozens of arrows, so many arrows that he had no chance of surviving. The hostile warriors did the same to Uncle Phil. Yemu and the others managed to get away and that's how we got the news of what happened.'

'Why couldn't Dad's body be found so he could have a grave?'

I looked at Mum's sorrowful face. 'There were no bodies. The hostile Yali were cannibals.'

Chapter 11

BIRTHDAYS AND DEATHDAYS

It was the best part of my school day to walk as fast as I possibly could out of the school gates and along the road, turn the corner, and halfway down the next street, run to number sixteen, where I'd burst through the back door and yell out, 'Mum!'

'Hello dear. How was your day?' she would always reply in a cheery voice.

But for some reason, not today.

'What's wrong?' I asked.

'I received some sad news from West Irian. A letter came from a missionary friend. I'll tell you about it later.'

I gave her a quick hug and went to find something to eat for afternoon tea.

When we had finished our evening meal, Mum told us all to stay at the table as she wanted to read the letter, which had arrived earlier in the day. She stood up and walked over to the marble-topped cabinet, picked up a thick envelope and returned to her chair. Trying not to cry, she pulled out the sheets of paper, and with a shaky voice, began to read.

'Dear Pat, it is with much heartache that I write to inform you of the tragic death of the Newman family and Meno Voth.'

My siblings and I gave a collective gasp and were shocked into silence.

She continued, 'On 31st December, pilot Meno Voth flew to Yasakor to pick up MAF missionaries Gene, Lois, Paul, Steven, Joyce and baby Jonathan and fly them to Mulia in the Central Highlands. As they flew towards the Baliem Valley, the weather suddenly changed for the worse and it wasn't long before they found themselves in dense clouds. Meno lost bearings and decided to descend to a lower altitude to see whether he could recognise any landmarks. Without realising it, he had flown his plane down into a narrow gorge. Radio contact with the base had failed and by the next day, there was still no word from Cessna PK MPH.

'A search party was organised and MAF scrambled all available planes to the area from where Meno had last reported. It was difficult to see anything in the wild terrain with its steep gorges but eventually, one of the MAF pilots saw wreckage belonging to a plane. Pat, you would not believe where the plane was found. It was way off course in the Seng Valley! No one could believe it was possible. The Newman family and Meno had crashed almost at the site where Stan and Phil had been murdered. The plane had caught fire and there was no sign of life.

'A helicopter was brought in to take missionaries Hank Worthington and Frank Clarke to the actual site of the crash.

There was great apprehension because we already knew what the natives in that area were capable of doing. To tell you the truth, Pat, we did not expect any survivors. Can you imagine the utter amazement when nine year old Paul Newman came running towards Hank? He was unharmed.

'Apparently, the plane had come too close to the side of a gorge and one wing hit a tree, causing the small Cessna to break up as it crashed to the ground. It then became engulfed in flames. No one made it out, except Paul. He had been sitting right at the back of the plane and as he saw the plane catch fire managed to unbuckle his seatbelt and crawl out of a hole in the fuselage. He had no idea where he was, much less knew it was near the village belonging to the cannibals who had murdered Stan and Phil.

Paul was able to fill Hank and the other missionaries in on some of the details regarding the crash. He also told them about the gentle care he received from one of the Yali men—Kusoho, who was against killing Stan and Phil and how Kusoho tried to keep him safe from the killers …'

Mum continued to read but I wasn't concentrating.

What's the point? I thought. *It doesn't make sense that so many people have to die. What about those nice little Newman children? Why did they have to die?* I couldn't understand the purpose of any of the deaths, including Dad and Uncle Phil's.

I went to my room, laid on the bed and stared at the plain white ceiling, tears slowly trickling from my eyes as I remembered the beautiful butterfly shaped cake that Aunt Lois Newman had made for my ninth birthday two months after my dad had been killed. Soon after that, Mum, Rod, Jan and I had flown out of West Irian to return to Australia, leaving behind every birthday and every deathday I'd known in my short life.

Some time later, Mum received another letter from one of her missionary colleagues in West Irian. This one contained more news about the situation with the Seng Valley Yali.

Mum's face told a different story after reading this letter. She explained that because of the plane crash and Kusoho caring for Paul, some of the missionaries were able to return to thank the people for not harming Paul. They gave gifts of axes and a pig to the killers in order to show them that they were forgiven for what they had done. My 'big brother', Luliap from Ninia, also went into the area with the missionaries to talk with the people of the Seng Valley. They told him of how sorry they were for killing Dad and Uncle Phil and said, 'Now we want someone to come and teach us about the new way.'

'I remember the night at Ninia when men were coming to kill us,' Mum added.

'What? You never told us that!'

'You children were asleep at the time and I didn't want to wake you until I knew more of the situation. It must have been around midnight when Arelek came running to tell me there was a large gathering of hostile men heading our way to kill us all. It was too late to reach anyone by radio and your dad was away on a trek, so I did the only thing I could do and that was pray. Obviously, I couldn't sleep and when the hours passed and nothing more seemed to be happening I went and found Arelek sitting outside and asked him what was going on? "Truly Nisingga, they were coming very close but suddenly stopped as if they'd seen something and all of them turned and ran away!"

'Well, this explains the mystery of that night.' Mum read the relevant section of the letter to us.

'One of the men from the hostile group told an amazing story. "One time we decided to go and kill the white family but when we got close to the duong's house we saw something that made us very afraid. There were huge men surrounding the house. We did not expect the house to be guarded so we changed our minds about killing the family and ran back the way we'd come."'

Mum smiled. 'I know there were no huge men with us that night at Ninia, only Arelek sitting on the steps outside! The Bible talks about angels and how God uses them as His messengers. Remember the verse in Psalm ninety one, "For He will command His angels concerning you to guard you in all your ways." I am confident that the angels were there with us on the night. It makes me realise that even though it was Dad, Uncle Phil, Meno Voth and the Newmans' time to leave this world, it wasn't time for the rest of us. God still has plans for us here and now!'

I must admit I wasn't all that interested in the progress that had been made with the hostile cannibals since my family left West Irian. Life back in Australia had its own problems, and in many ways was even more alien to me than where I grew up with the Yali in Ninia.

The dreaded day had arrived. It was the day of the school's swimming carnival! Living in a place surrounded by mountains over 2,000 metres high with only a raging river at their base, doesn't give a person the opportunity to learn to swim. Mum must have thought I had the capability, especially after she'd enrolled me in a few swimming lessons at the local pool and had signed the permission slip for me to participate in the carnival. This was all the authority the teacher needed to insist I get into the pool and swim in the twenty-five metre freestyle event.

The students were divided into four teams—Bass, Hume, Flinders and Hovell, the names of well-known Australian explorers. I felt sick in my stomach and to make matters worse, did not have a single friend to sit with in the bleachers. I waited for the dreaded moment when I would be called on to take my place in the line-up and at the same time thinking, *I wish a modern day miracle would happen and the pool is emptied of water.*

I felt a nudge to my ribs by a girl seated next to me and looked up to see the teacher was heading my way with the obligatory clipboard in hand. 'Dale, you're in this race for Hovell. Go to the pool!' With pleading eyes, I looked up at the teacher, but her attention was long gone.

Walking slowly to the edge of the watery grave, I took my stand next to the other competitors. The loud shrill of a whistle sounded and I belly flopped into the wetness—I barely knew how to swim, let alone dive!

The only thing in my favour that fateful morning was that I had been allocated the outside lane. Floundering and gasping for air like a fish thrown onto a boat's waterless deck, I kept my left hand close to the wall while trying to use my right hand to propel myself forward through the choppy water. The panic I felt when seated in the bleachers had now graduated to a new level. I was in serious trouble. Not having goggles meant keeping my eyes tightly shut as I groped wildly for the security of the pool's wall. Somehow I managed to hold on and slide myself awkwardly through the water until my rising panic called it a day and my race came to an abrupt stop.

Holding onto the side with my head down, I heard the teacher. 'Dale, get out of the pool.' My gratitude to her was immense. It never occurred to me that she probably didn't want a case of drowning on her hands! I slunk back to my spot on the hard planks, water dripping miserably off my shaking body. *Never again*, I thought. Already the plan was forming in my mind of how to get out of any future swimming carnivals.

I made no friends for the remainder of my primary school years, at least not at school. My only real friendship was formed with a neighbourhood girl who lived four houses along the street from me. Jenny and I would spend hours together, either at her home or mine, until Mum, much to my embarrassment would say, 'Run along home now, dear. You've been here long enough.'

My first year of 'white' school was the most frightening time of my life and I only opened my mouth at school to exhale, nibble nervously on a vegemite sandwich, and drink the milk from the small glass bottle that had been sitting in a crate out in the school yard all morning. Every student had to drink one third of a pint of milk—no excuses!

I'd never been to a school before and had no idea what I was supposed to do or say to all these strangers who talked of things I knew nothing about and each day I would beg my mother not to send me back to 'that place'.

I knew of no one whose parent had died and divorce wasn't common, so the dilemma of me coming from a single parent home was a tricky one. Did I try to explain to the other kids at school why I only have a mum? No, they'd never believe the reason I'd give anyway. It was bad enough that I was already the odd one out from only having the one parent. There was no way anyone would believe me if I told them my dad had been murdered by cannibals!

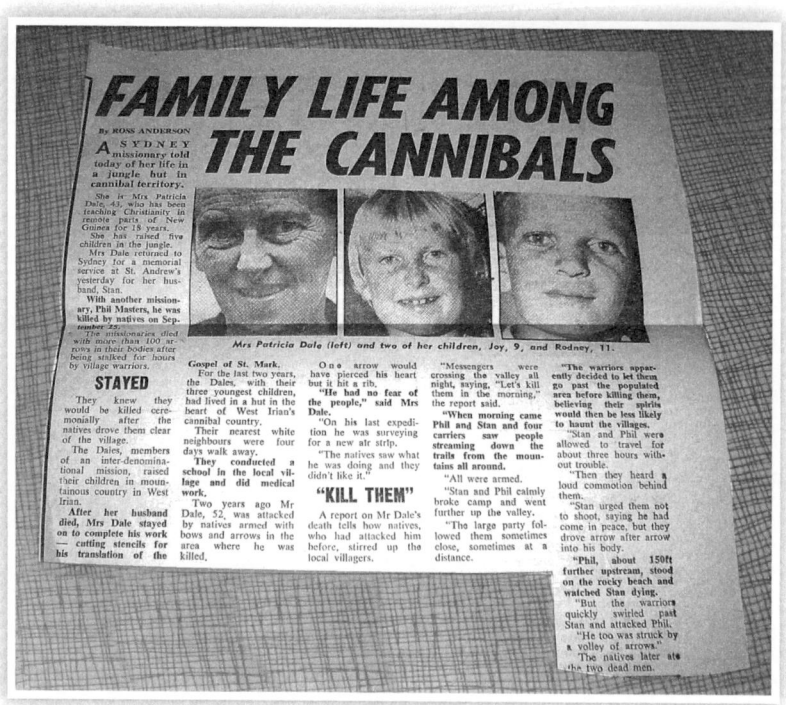

Newspaper article

I kept my mouth shut, avoiding awkward questions.

When I was older I overheard two strangers talking about how they thought it was wrong of missionaries to go into other cultures and try and change the people. 'It's not right to interfere in someone else's life and try to change their culture.'

'Yeah, that's what those crazy missionary people do. I mean, who do they think they are, going to places where people have had their own customs and beliefs for centuries?'

'Primitive cultures should be left intact. No one's got the right to impose their belief system on others.'

I was shocked after hearing these comments. To think that people would criticise us for going to the Yali, knowing the sacrifice we made in giving up a comfortable life in Australia, to live in one of the most primitive places in the world, in order to help people and bring a message of hope to them!

Don't others understand how horrible some people's lives are? I thought. *Don't they realise that everyone in this world should have an opportunity for a better life? Would they put up with the conditions the Yali lived in? Do they accept that it's okay for women to be abused and children put to death for something they did in innocence? Would they like it if they had no medicine or medical help for their loved ones and had to watch them die before their eyes?*

The Yali lived in fear and repression and with no understanding that there could be a better way to live, and of course, the 'big' question for me was: *don't people see any wrong in the fact that some human beings actually kill and eat each other?*

'Your word is a lamp to my feet and a light for my path.'
Psalm 119:105

Chapter 12
THE BEGINNING

By the time I'd reached high school the bullying I'd experienced changed to a greater level of meanness. 'Eww, hold your nose, here comes "stale dale"!'

A scuffed shoe reached out to trip me over. Thankfully, I'd made time to eat breakfast that morning which must have helped in giving me the quick thinking necessary to avoid what would have been an uncomfortable landing on the hard linoleum floor.

Whether it was a moment of triumph or madness I don't know, but I looked at bully number three from 'the gang' and did the unthinkable. I poked my tongue out! He responded with a faintly surprised look before smirking and walking off in the opposite direction.

I sighed softly and thought of how my personality must seem to others. I was the quiet, shy girl from a poor, single-parent family and someone to be either pitied or provoked.

My school reports all reflected the same sentiment, 'Joy is a quiet student who tries hard.' Outwardly, it seemed as if people's summary of me was correct, but I knew another 'me'! This one had imagination, a sense of humour, steely determination and an unquenchable interest in life outside the borders of just one country.

Dreaming of travelling the world prompted me to pick up an application form for the Australian navy. 'Mum, would you please sign this form for me?'

'What's it about?'

'I want to join the navy but because I'm under eighteen you need to sign it.' 'Absolutely not! You're not going into the navy,' replied my stunned Mother.

After a time of pleading and making a case for how wonderful it would be to explore the world, I stomped off realising that my future plans were being derailed.

If only she'd signed the navy application form instead of the school's swimming carnival note. To me, joining the navy was a far less frightening option!

A highlight in my teenage years was going to youth group at church. Every Saturday night I looked forward to an evening of fun and encouraging talks. I'd even managed to make a few friends there. We had a terrific youth leader named Ian Purse, or 'Pursey', as he was affectionately known. He went out of his way to be kind and caring to everyone, including me.

One night, there was a visiting speaker. We all found a place to sit on the carpet and the noisy chatter and laughter died down.

A young man in his early twenties moved towards the front and waited for silence. He hesitated, as if being prompted by someone, and then began talking.

'Hi, guys. It's great to be here with you all tonight. My name is Jeff and I've come to talk to you about probably the most commonly asked question in life. Why does bad stuff happen?'

My head snapped up. *You're a genius if you've got the answer to that!* The speaker continued,

'Most people at some point in life ask this question. I know I have, especially after what happened to me. Almost two years ago on a Friday night, my sister, who was sixteen, was going to meet some friends at the movies and asked me if I could give her a ride.

'I said, "Sure, it's not like I've got anything better to do." We drove off from our house and were talking and laughing. We only had about two blocks to go before we reached the cinema. The lights at the intersection had just turned green, so I kept driving through at the speed limit.

'The next thing I remember was the sound of crunching metal and smashing glass and a feeling came over me like I was in some kind of a dream.

'When I woke up in a hospital bed with my left leg in a plaster cast and scratches and bruises everywhere on my body, the realisation dawned that I'd been in a car accident. Suddenly I remembered my sister.' He paused before continuing, 'I looked at my parents, who stood up from their chairs when they saw I had woken and I could see the answer in their swollen, red-rimmed eyes. My sister had been killed.'

By this time the room had become silent and I sat there wondering what to do with this news. Jeff went on. 'We had been hit by a drunk driver who ran a red light. I still can't fully believe that my sister is gone. She was the happiest, brightest, most caring person I've ever known.

'I screamed out to God, "Why did you let this happen?"

'Soon after that, I went into a deep depression which lasted around six months. Although I believed in God, I wasn't a Christian at that time. I was pretty full of myself and thought I had all the answers to life but after the accident, came to realise I didn't have any. Yeah, so it was a selfish person driving a car when they were drunk that got my little sister killed, but couldn't God have stopped the guy from getting into his car? Couldn't the driver have gone a different route that night?

'I couldn't figure out why bad things happen to innocent 'good' people. What about when a baby dies or someone gets cancer or people are killed in a natural disaster? Couldn't God stop all that from happening? The question kept eating away at me and it didn't help that I was constantly depressed.

'One day, a friend came to see me and he told me that he was concerned for me and asked if there was anything he could do. I just looked at him and burst into tears and couldn't stop crying. Finally, when I could speak a little I asked, "Why is life so unfair?"

'My friend was a Christian and what he said to me is what I want to tell you all tonight. It's not often you hear people say things like, "Why am I blessed with more than enough food and clothes and have good health and a nice home?" No, most of us say things like, "Why am I allergic to wheat? Why do my friends have heaps better stuff than me? Why do people have to get a terminal illness?" This negative "why" question, is not a new one. We only have to read the Bible to see that this question was asked repeatedly.

'The Bible talks about a man named Job. Job was a righteous man, committed to doing good, yet God allowed him to go through incredible trials. He lost his wealth, his family, his health. It got to a point where Job said to God, "Why did I not perish at birth, and die as I came from the womb?" Job was so overcome with his suffering that he wished he'd never been born!

'One of the main writers of the book of Psalms is a guy named David and he was constantly questioning God. "How long, O Lord? Will you forget me forever? How long will you hide your face from me? How long will I wrestle with my thoughts and every day have sorrow in my heart? How long will my enemy triumph over me?"

'I have often heard people say, "If God is loving, why does He allow so much suffering?" It seems like an open and shut case to many. They won't accept a God who could prevent suffering but often doesn't. For those of us who are Christians, what happens to our faith, if we've asked God to protect our loved ones and they aren't protected?'

Now the speaker had my complete attention! *Wasn't this what happened to Dad and Uncle Phil and the Newman family and their pilot, Meno Voth? I remember before Dad and Uncle Phil set off on their final trek our families sat down together for lunch and then prayed for safety for all of us. Didn't God hear our prayer? He obviously 'dropped the ball' on that one!*

But then it hit me. Hundreds, if not thousands, of Yali people had come to know about God's love and forgiveness due to Dad, Uncle Phil and the others giving up their earthly lives. The 'why' in this situation had been answered for me and my family long ago. I just failed to see it.

Jeff continued, 'Sometimes you may hear people ask, "Why didn't God create a world where there was no suffering or pain?" In Genesis chapter one, you will read that what God created was originally perfect. Then sin came into the world and all that 'goodness' changed. God gave people a free will and Adam and Eve used their free to make a choice to disobey God. As a result, the once perfect world became a fallen world.'

Yes, I thought. *It was sin that was responsible for my dad's death.*

He was murdered by people who followed a way of life that was wrong. How could it be possible that killing someone and eating them was a 'right' thing to do? Who on earth would say that throwing a small, defenceless child into a raging river and letting them drown, just because that child innocently touched or did something that was considered sacred, was acceptable or right?

Jeff went on,

'God can use the bad that happens in our lives and turn it into good. God can use our suffering to help us become better people if we trust Him. We are not defined by the negative things that come our way. We're defined by what God says about us. The bullies will bully, hard times will come, we may feel like giving up, but we mustn't forget who has the last word.

'One day this life will be over. The Bible makes that clear. "Heaven and earth will pass away but my words will never pass away." What we go through now in this life—the good, the bad and the ugly, is all coming to an end. The important thing for us to remember in the meantime though is that we make a choice. When the bad stuff happens, we can either turn to God or turn away from Him. As someone once said, "We can become bitter or we can become better."

'My Christian friend was a great help in getting me to understand this. He told me that God loved me so much that he sent His only son to die for me, to take the punishment for my sins and provide a way for me to know peace in this life even when bad things happen.

'We also get to have the most amazing gift ever—eternal life!

'For those of us who place our faith and trust in God, whatever happens to us in life, we do not go through it alone. God promises to go with us. The tragedies and struggles will still come. No one goes through life without bad things happening to them at some point. I want to encourage you all here tonight to think about the things my friend told me and to commit your lives to a loving heavenly Father who understands all your pain and hurt. He has a plan for your life that will ultimately make sense.'

My mind wandered again to life in PNG or Irian Jaya as the place was now called. It was where I first heard about Jesus from my dad and where I got to know the Yali people, whose lives were full of sadness and fear, but because of the great sacrifice of others, they got to hear about Jesus. Now many of the Yali people were enjoying true peace for the first time. More importantly, they had a certainty about their eternal future.

It seemed surreal to think about the way Dad and Uncle Phil had died. There was a part of me that blocked out the horror and I realised it must have been God who gave me the ability to view everything from the sideline and not take on board the shocking nature of the death of both dads. It was as if God had put a protective hedge around me so I wouldn't have to think about something that was too terrible to bear.

Mum had also mentioned that many people from around the world had prayed for our family. There's no doubt this helped us.

Jeff was coming to the end of his talk.

'There may be someone here tonight who has already got to the point of wanting to trust that God is still in control of this crazy, mixed-up world we live in and recognise that His ways are not always our ways. You might be longing to have peace in your life and to know with certainty that someone "has your back", to save you from living a life full of anger and pain. If that's you and you want to go further in trusting God, could I lead you in a prayer right now?'

I'd heard the gospel message all my life, having come from a missionary background, and so I thought I was okay when it came to spiritual matters. However, this talk touched a nerve in me. I needed to make a decision for myself, not one based on my parents' or anyone else's faith.

I bowed my head and prayed along with Jeff.

I left youth group that night with a lighter, happier heart than I'd had for a long time, maybe even since my life with the Yali. Although things were different for me and I'd had to learn to live all over again in a new culture, I began to realise that the God I'd heard about from the day I was born was the same God I heard about that night.

Everything in life can change in an instant, whether through tragedy or circumstances beyond our control, but that doesn't mean God has abandoned us, even though we may feel He has. The problem often comes when we rely on our feelings instead of God's truth and that's why it's important to understand *who* God is.

It had taken a long time for me to understand that I mattered to God. I was loved by Him as much as anyone else was loved. I may not have both my parents and the opportunities other kids my age had in life, but that didn't mean I was less worthy or less important in God's eyes.

Of course my problems didn't magically melt away because I had become a Christian, but it meant I had a mighty arsenal of weapons at my disposal with which to fight my problems. Not the kind of weapons the Yali had with their bows, arrows, crude axes and superstitious beliefs, but a weapon that could conquer anything—the help of Jesus Christ; God who became man. He understands my pain, anger, disappointment, regrets and sadness. He provides a way through the dark times in my life.

> For I am convinced that neither death nor life, neither angels nor demons, neither the present nor the future, nor any powers, neither height nor depth, nor anything else in all creation, will be able to separate us from the love of God that is in Christ Jesus our Lord. (Romans 8:38,39)

God loves me no matter what has happened in my past or what is happening right now or what will happen in the future. He can work everything out for my good. If I keep trusting in Him, life will make sense, maybe not always in this alien world, but most certainly in the eternal life to come.

> 'At Allah en di ap homi su ap homi mundoho enelaheg neg bebag ma, at amloho ilahambi henenda nobam dip-nobaharuk kahep halug, elehapdoho henobahaku fug Henoluk mundoho welamuhup on hwelahup en og-hesasi.' Yohanes 3:16

> (For God so loved the world that he gave his one and only Son, that whoever believes in him shall not perish but have eternal life.' John 3:16)

Luliap, Joy and Otto many years after the events of this story

THE BEGINNING

Pat Dale died 11th June 2006, exactly forty years to the day after the martyrdom of Yeikwaroho and Bingguok, her two Yali 'sons'.

Dale family 2005

Yeikwaroho preaching at Ninia

A special mention must go to:

My siblings
Rod and Jan
who lived the Ninia story with me daily
and
Wes and Hil
who, for the most part, lived it from a distance

My family
Mark, Luke, Joel and Amy
who never allow me to give up

AND

My Yali friends
who are forever in my heart

Nenda hundik humdoho henepuk kahi
(I love you VERY much)

Yemu playing his binggong in the late 1990's.

'My heart is steadfast, O God;
I will sing and make music with all my soul.
Awake, harp and lyre!
I will awaken the dawn.
I will praise you, O LORD, among the nations;
I will sing of you among the peoples.
For great is your love, higher than the heavens;
Your faithfulness reaches to the skies.
Be exalted, O God, above the heavens,
and let your glory be over all the earth.'

Psalm 108:1-5

AUTHOR'S NOTE

25/09/2016
On the 40th anniversary of my dad's martyrdom I felt compelled to commemorate the occasion in some way so I commenced writing a book. However the project stalled and took a back seat for over seven years until earlier this year when I was prompted to begin writing again. Now eight months later the goal has been achieved.

 In a modern world where the emphasis is on 'right here, right now', it can be frustrating to slow down and wait patiently for things to happen. As a Christian I've had to learn—often the hard way—that my plans are not always the same as God's plans for me. Whenever I look back though and see how God has reworked the 'negative' for 'positive' it's given me a greater ability to trust Him. It also gives me a better understanding of the fact that I only see, at any given time, one small section of this huge puzzle called, 'life'. I may never get the answer to every 'why' question, but what gives me peace is knowing that God has the answers and He is faithful and good because He has proved Himself to be so…

ACKNOWLEDGEMENTS

No book comes together without the involvement of others and as such I must give thanks to:

Lynne Stringer—for your editorial assistance. If not for you I'd still be stuck in chronological chaos! Your experience and expertise in the written world is much admired.

Joy Lankshear—such a talented graphic designer. You captured my vision for the book cover so well.

Mark Crawford, Janet Dale, Cindy Bissett, Luke Crawford, Adele Smith, Amy Crawford and 'Yalihwe' (Carol Clark)—my determined proof readers. I appreciate you setting aside time in your busy lives to help me with this big task.

Joel Crawford, Steph Wilson, Sam Fry, Patrick Stubbs—my willing test subjects. Your feedback on a book which has been written primarily for your age group has been encouraging.

Ian Purse—my 'ageless' youth pastor—who better to write a Foreword—your care and concern for youth spans more than four decades, impacting countless lives for good, including mine.

Hoerlina Pahabol, Art, Carol, Don, Nate and Leigh Clark, and the late Henggry Balingga—my gracious translators. I'm grateful to you for bringing me up to speed on some of the Yali language and customs. Wa! wa!

This is the tract that completely changed Stan Dale's life

FOUR THINGS GOD WANTS YOU TO KNOW

1. You need to be saved from sin's penalty

All we like sheep have gone astray; we have turned everyone to his own way. (Isaiah 53:6)

There is a way that seems right to a man, but its end is the way to death. (Proverbs 14:12)

For all have sinned, and fall short of the glory of God. (Romans 3:23)

The wages of sin is death. (Romans 6:23)

Each of us will give an account of himself to God. (Romans 14:12)

It is appointed for man to die once, and after that comes judgement. (Hebrews 9:27)

2. You cannot save yourself

Unless one is born again he cannot see the kingdom of God. (John 3:3)

He saved us, not because of works done by us in righteousness, but according to his own mercy. (Titus 3:5)

For whoever keeps the whole law but fails in one point has become accountable for all of it. (James 2:10)

Jesus said to him, 'I am the way, and the truth, and the life. No one comes to the Father except through me.' (John 14:6)

3. Jesus has provided for your salvation

For there is one God, and there is one mediator between God and men, the man Christ Jesus. (1 Timothy 2:5)

For Christ also suffered once for sins, the righteous for the unrighteous, that he might bring us to God. (1 Peter 3:18)

For our sake he [God] made him [Jesus] to be sin who knew no sin, so that in him we might become the righteousness of God. (2 Corinthians 5:21)

God so loved the world, that he gave his only Son, that whoever believes in him should not perish but have eternal life. (John 3:16)

4. You can be saved today

Whoever hears my word and believes has passed from death to life. (John 5:24)

Behold, now is the … time; behold, now is the day of salvation. (2 Corinthians 6:2)

Seek the Lord while he may be found, call upon him while he is near. (Isaiah 55:6)

Your part:

Believe:
Believe in the Lord Jesus, and you will be saved. (Acts 16:31)

Repent (turn from your sins):
Unless you repent, you will all likewise perish. (Luke 13:3)

Confess your sin to Jesus:
For there is one God, and there is one mediator between God and men, the man Christ Jesus. (1 Timothy 2:5)

Confess Jesus before others:
If you confess with your mouth that Jesus is Lord and believe in your heart that God raised him from the dead, you will be saved. (Romans 10:9)

Trust Him to keep you:
[He] is able to keep you from stumbling. (Jude 24)

That's what God wants you to know!

TO THINK ABOUT

Chapter 1
Not everyone can go to a far-flung place to be a missionary so how can we be a missionary right where we are?
See Acts 9:36; 1 Peter 3:15

Chapter 2
What are some ways in which God reveals Himself to people?
See Psalm 19:1-4; Romans 1:18-20; John 3:16

Chapter 3
Do you think God has favourites? Why do some people seem to 'have it all' while others struggle to even live?
See Romans 9:14-16; Psalm 73; Acts 10:34-35

Chapter 4
What do you think about the statement, 'Only one life, it will soon be past, only what's done for Christ will last?'
See 2 Corinthians 4:18; James 4:13-17

Chapter 5
What do you think is the most important quality for a person to have and why?
See 1 Corinthians 13

Chapter 6
What can we do when we feel like giving up?
See Isaiah 41:10; Galatians 6:9; Matthew 11:28; Joshua 1:9

Chapter 7
What can modern day idols (things that take us away from God) look like?
See Exodus 20:3; Matthew 6:24

Chapter 8
Do you think there's such a thing as 'coincidence' for a Christian?
See Proverbs 19:21; Isaiah 46:9-11; Matthew 10:29; Romans 8:28

Chapter 9
How would you describe sin?
See Romans 3:23; Colossians 3:8-14; 1 John 3:4; Isaiah 53:6

Chapter 10
When bad stuff happens it can be easy to doubt God's existence. What can we do if we feel this way?
See Psalm 40:1-2; Psalm 62:8; John 14:27; 1 Peter 5:7; James 4:7-8

Chapter 11

If we are going through tough times, what is the first thing we can do?

See Psalm 145:18; Proverbs 3:5-6; Romans 12:12; Philippians 4:6-7

Chapter 12

'When we understand who God is, we will understand what He does.'

What do you think this quote means?

See 2 Chronicles 20:6; Psalm 18:30; Psalm 115:3; Isaiah 40:28; Isaiah 55:8

If you take only one thought away from this book, remember this—even when our 'why' questions are not answered, God has not stopped loving us and He has not given up on us.